Dwapara Yuga and Yogananda:
Blueprint for a New Age

For my good friend Sven,

Simon

Jan '08

By
Poor Richard

**"Wherever you see ashes, throw it up,
you might just get the priceless gem!"**

Swami Sri Yukteswar

Table of Contents

Acknowledgements

Everything in this book comes from the Kriya Yoga Line of Gurus[1] whose selfless energy brought long-forgotten Indian knowledge back for Dwapara Yuga. The author is proud to be an American. The sacrifices of the Founding Fathers, military and citizens have created a legacy of freedom both in the United States and around the world for which the author is truly grateful. After all, a poor, oppressed person is hardly free to ponder philosophical questions, instead focused to the next meal or state handout.

A debt of gratitude is owed to Swami Kriyananda for the clarity of his writings and to his example of "World Brotherhood Colonies" around the world. Paramhansa[2] Yogananda quotes his guru Sri Yukteswar thus in the "Autobiography of a Yogi":

"Why are you averse to organizational work?"

Master's question startled me a bit. It is true that my private conviction at the time was that organizations were "hornets' nests."

"It is a thankless task, sir," I answered. "No matter what the leader does or does not, he is criticized."

"Do you want the whole divine channa (milk curd) for yourself alone?" My guru's retort was accompanied by a stern glance.

"Could you or anyone else achieve God-contact through yoga if a line of generous-hearted masters had not been willing to convey their knowledge to others?" He added, "God is the Honey, organizations are the hives; both are necessary. Any form is useless, of course, without the spirit, but why should you not start busy hives full of the spiritual nectar?"

After all it was the 1893 (193 Dwapara) World's Parliament of Religions in Chicago that marked the first formal gathering of representatives of Eastern and Western spiritual traditions (also the year of

---

1 See the chapter "Kriya Yoga Line of Gurus"

[2] The Bengali word Paramhansa, meaning "Great Swan", is written Paramahansa in Sanskrit. Yogananda used the Bengali form during his lifetime.

Yogananda's birth).   Today it is recognized as the occasion of the birth of formal interreligious dialog worldwide.

The eloquence of Swami Vivekananda (student of Sri Ramakrishna) and his introduction of Hindu thought to the United States are particularly remembered.   The speech has been identified by many to mark the beginning of western interest in Hinduism.   His opening line, "Sisters and Brothers of America..." was greeted by a three minute standing ovation from the audience.

The 1920 (220 Dwapara) International Congress of Free Christians and Other Religious Liberals in Boston introduced (then) Swami Yogananda to the West.   Both meetings were expansive beyond the narrow confines of any one organization.   I would also like to thank Wikipedia, for making it so simple to stand on the shoulders of giants and to the Economist Magazine, National Public Radio, and the Wall Street Journal for their excellent coverage of world affairs.

Author's Preface

Dwapara Yuga can be characterized as a breakdown of the idea of a material world and a growing consciousness of the underlying unity of peoples, energy and nature. This short book is a "Poor Richard's Almanac"[3] for a New Age.

It was developed on an Apple iMac as a blog[4] using blogger.com with the goal of inviting comment and collaboration. Any profits from this book will be donated to the One Laptop per Child Foundation (laptopfoundaton.org), which aims to bridge the digital divide in the developing world either directly with its specially created laptops, or in spurring giants such as Microsoft or Intel into action. The views are the author's own and not those of any other individual or organization.

Introduction

This short book deals with two intertwined stories: that of the New Age of Dwapara Yuga and the life of Paramhansa Yogananda, the Indian Yogi who brought that knowledge to the West, his teachers and those who he influenced.

Merriam Webster's Dictionary defines New Age as an eclectic group of cultural attitudes arising in late 20th century Western society that are adapted from those of a variety of ancient and modern cultures, that emphasize beliefs (as reincarnation, holism, pantheism, and occultism) outside the mainstream, and that advance alternative approaches to spirituality, right living and health. According to a 1996 survey[5]:

98% of Americans believe in God
20% of Americans are "New Agers"

The West has always had secret or mystery schools practicing astrology, alchemy, Kabbalah and even magic but these were historically not widely known and open only to elites since the oppressive nature of monarchy, aristocracy, organized religion and various

---

[3] Poor Richard's Almanac was a yearly almanac published by Benjamin Franklin, who adopted the pseudonym of "Poor Richard" for this purpose. The publication appeared continuously from 1732 to 1758.

[4] Dwaparayuga.com

[5] George Barnia, "The Index of Leading Spiritual Indicators", Word Publishing, Dallas TX, 1996

collectivisms such as national and communist socialism relied upon conformism and lack of creativity among the populace.

Yogananda became the most popular speaker in the United States in the 1920s and 30s, crisscrossing the country to speak to filled-to-capacity auditoria, having the ear of leading figures such as the President, the Governor of California, Burbank, Ford and Edison. He brought an ancient message of simple living and high thinking to a new audience, emphasizing healthy diet, exercise and meditation at a time when these ideas were far from common. Most of all he emphasized the personal contact with God, without priestly intermediary: how to make a Christian, a better Christian, a Jew, a better Jew and so on.

When Yogananda began using mass media to disseminate his message he was building on foundations laid in the 19th century by the Adventist, Latter Day Saints (LDS or Mormon) and Unity Churches as well as the Transcendentalist, Spiritualist, Mesmerist and Theosophical movements that had begun questioning the monolithic nature of established thought and institutions, in effect applying Jesus' teaching below:

> Then Jesus said to the crowds and to his disciples: "The teachers of the law and the Pharisees sit in Moses' seat. So you must obey them and do everything they tell you. But do not do what they do, for they do not practice what they preach. They tie up heavy loads and put them on men's shoulders, but they themselves are not willing to lift a finger to move them.
>
> "Everything they do is done for men to see: They make their phylacteries wide and the tassels on their garments long; they love the place of honor at banquets and the most important seats in the synagogues; they love to be greeted in the marketplaces and to have men call them 'Rabbi.'[6]

When the Pilgrims first came to America in 1620, they had first to agree on how to live together in the Mayflower Compact, the first step towards an American Constitution and a step away from the tyranny of so-called Nobility and Organized Religion.

Their emphasis on reading the Bible, rather than relying on the interpretations of religious leaders, lead to widespread literacy and by the time of de

---

[6] Matthew 23:1-12, NIV

Tocqueville, two centuries later, he found along with the Bible:

> "There is hardly a pioneer's hut that does not contain a few odd volumes of Shakespeare. I remember that I read the feudal drama of Henry V for the first time in a log cabin."

From the 1940s, Yogananda concentrated on writing, saying that after his death the writings would be the teacher, anticipating the organizational squabbles[7] to come. This book draws heavily on Yogananda's writings, those of his teacher Swami Sri Yukteswar and Yogananda's disciples.

The present book is not meant to be a restatement of Yogananda's teachings, concentrating only on the kernel of his message and the more obscure aspects of his teachings, especially in regard to Dwapara Yuga. His Kriya Yoga meditation techniques are not described here. Many organizations[8] in the US teach them since they are practical rather than theoretical exercises. In terms of the Yugas, the emphasis is on the unfolding of Dwapara Yuga and not on past higher ages, astronomy or archeology since these are well covered in other books[9].

It is the author's hope that the diligent reader will come away with a broad understanding of Dwapara Yuga, Yogananda's mission and what developments we are likely to see as we move into the fullest expression of Dwapara Yuga. Sufficient reference material has been provided to kick-start a deeper personal research, unlimited by the constraints of any particular organization.

> "Then you will know the truth and the truth will set you free."[10]

---

[7] Please refer to the chapter "Organizational Squabbles"
[8] Please refer to the chapter "Major Kriya Yoga Organizations in the United States".
[9] Please refer to the website "Conference on Precession and Ancient Knowledge". Cpakonline.com
[10] John 8:32, NIV

Dwapara Yuga

Explanation

In 1894, Swami Sri Yukteswar made two startling predictions based on ancient Indian writings in his book "the Holy Science": "matter will be found to be energy" and "our sun has a twin star". Einstein proved the first prediction true in 1905 and over the course of the last century it has been found that two out of every three stars is part of a binary system[11].

Sri Yukteswar writes that as well as the daily rotation of the Earth on its axis and yearly journey around the sun, the sun itself orbits another star, with a period of about 24,000 years. The rotation of the earth relative to the stars we see (the zodiac in astrological terms) is called the precession of the equinoxes. Modern science agrees with the period yet offers an alternate explanation: that of the earth's wobble on its axis.

Many ancient sites are constructed with elements demonstrating very sophisticated astronomical knowledge. For example, the orientation of the shafts on certain ancient pyramids can be read as date-stamps.

Sri Yukteswar described the orbit, as moving the earth in an ascending arc of 12,000 years, raising the consciousness of man, and then a falling arc of 12,000 years, lowering it, as the earth approaches and then recedes from a galactic center called Vishnunabhi. Each arc is called a Daiba Yuga or Electric Cycle. One day of Brahma is the time taken for one thousand cycles of Daibas. A day of Brahama is followed by the night of Brahma. The Earth is many days and nights of Brahma old.

The Greeks and many other ancient cultures (for example: Egyptians, Persians, Sumerians, Aztecs, Hopi, Celts and Norse) shared this idea of the ages of man. The Greeks called the phenomenon the Great Year. The Hindu ages or Yugas are summarized below, with their Greek equivalents. Like all things in nature, the transitions are gradual, with a Sandhi or transition period at the beginning and end of each age.

---

[11] January 10, 2006, "Planetary systems can form around binary stars", Dr. Alan Boss at the American Astronomical Society meeting in Washington, DC.

Yuga	Greek Age	Characteristics
Satya	Gold	Harmony with the Divine plan
Treta	Silver	Time-Annihilation
Dwapara	Bronze	Space-Annihilation
Kali	Iron	Materialism and ignorance

Arc	Yuga	Length	Sandhi	From	To
Descending	Satya	4800	400	11500 BC	6700 BC
	Treta	3600	300	6700 BC	3100 BC
	Dwapara	2400	200	3100 BC	700 BC
	Kali	1200	100	700 BC	500 AD
Ascending	Kali	1200	100	500 AD	1700 AD
	Dwapara	2400	200	1700 AD	4100 AD
	Treta	3600	300	4100 AD	7700 AD
	Satya	4800	400	7700 AD	12500 AD

From the fall of Rome, around 500 AD, to the Renaissance, ten to twelve centuries later, almost nothing new was discovered. Man looked back to the great learning of classical civilization for inspiration: admiring their thinkers and architects but incapable of equaling them. In turn, those ancients looked back further, to a previous "Golden Age."

As can be seen, the low point of human consciousness was 500 AD marked by ignorance and destruction. From approximately 1600 to 1900 AD, we have been transitioning to Dwapara Yuga, the Bronze Age. The highest point of the last highest Satya or Golden Age was 11500 BC.

Sri Yukteswar proposed reviving the ancient dating convention relative to the age, for example:

- 500 AD becomes 0 Kali since it is the dawn of Ascending Kali Yuga.
- 1200 AD becomes 700 Kali since it is 700 years after 0 Kali.
- 1700 AD becomes 0 Dwapara since it is the dawn of Ascending Dwapara Yuga.
- 2007 AD becomes 307 Dwapara since it is 307 years after 0 Dwapara.

Yogananda published Sri Yukteswar's book in the United States. Yogananda's student, Tara Mata, wrote a commentary in 1933 called "Astrological World Cycles" and Yogananda broached the subject in his 1946 "Autobiography of a Yogi". The idea of Yugas was somewhat known since the Theosophists had documented them since the 1870s but without the insight of Sri Yukteswar and his correction of the erroneous calculations.

This interpretation by Sri Yukteswar is at odds with the Orthodox Hindu interpretation, under which we are still in the age of Kali Yuga, rather than Dwapara Yuga. The explanation is simple: during Kali Yuga man was not capable of interpreting the texts written in higher ages.

In 1900 Swami Sri Yukteswar had made a procession in Serampore to celebrate the full expression of Dwapara Yuga (200 years being the transition period for full expression from 1700, 0 Dwapara). His procession was little understood and stones were thrown since his views did not represent traditional dogma.

Similarly, the Astrologers in the West speak of entering an "Age of Aquarius" but their calculations are similarly incorrect. Their detection of dawning of a New Age is itself accurate, along with many of the aspect of Dwapara and higher ages, joyously summarized in the 1969 hit "Aquarius" from the musical "Hair" – "Harmony and understanding, Sympathy and trust abounding, No more falsehoods or derisions, Golden living dreams of visions".

Dwapara Yuga, fully expressed in 1900, can be characterized as a breakdown of the idea of a material world and a growing consciousness of the underlying unity of peoples, energy and nature, manifesting in:

- Understanding of finer energies and structure of universe
- Freedom of
    - Speech
    - Travel and communication
    - Sharing and community of all kinds
    - Acquisition and access to all knowledge
    - Consumption and creation of media of all forms
- End of Mayic/Demonic/Satanic powers
  (in the sense of limiting/obstructing the individual) of
    - Aristocracy
    - Authoritarianism
    - Autocracy
    - Cartels
    - Collectivism
    - Communist Socialism
    - Cronyism

- o Dictatorship
- o Kleptocracy
- o Mafiosi
- o Matriarchy
- o Monarchy
- o Monopolies
- o National Socialism
- o Nepotism
- o Oligarchy
- o Patriarchy
- o Petromonarchy
- o Slavery
- o Technocracy
- o Theocracy
- o Totalitarianism
- End of discrimination by
  - o Age
  - o Caste
  - o Class
  - o Gender
  - o Geography
  - o Health
  - o Race
  - o Religion
  - o Wealth
- Free trade, globalization, capitalism, meritocracy, equality, freedom and democracy
- Empowerment of the individual, rise of a middle class, strength thru diversity

The rich wield financial, political and social power, controlling countries overtly or covertly, the poor have nothing and the middle class are somewhere in between. In third world countries, there tend only to be rich and poor. One sign of the development of a country is how much of a middle class it has and whether it is growing or shrinking, gaining or lessening in financial, political and social power. Today in the United States, the top 5% of the population have more wealth than the remaining 95% combined[12], a situation that was last repeated just prior to the 1929 Crash.

Politicians, inventors and thinkers who are in line with Dwapara Yuga ideas have flourished and been feted. Those who opposed them had limited or only

---

[12] Edward Wolff, professor of economics at New York University, author of Top Heavy: The Increasing Inequality of Wealth in America

short-lived success. Paramhansa Yogananda explained the mechanism for the Yugas: ideas are tuned-into by great minds rather than being created by them. These ideas in turn drive great civilizations. The United States best exemplifies outer freedom where someone not a king, nor noble, nor well-born can achieve any material success. India best exemplifies inner freedom thru meditation. Yogananda proposed a future with a best of America's "can do" attitude and India's inner mental hygiene.

Interestingly Yogananda explains that the success of the United States is not due to its scientific and technological supremacy rather the good karma of its religious population and foundation along spiritual principles, in sharp contrast to Latin America, founded for the exploitation of resources.

He predicted that the joining of the United States of America, United States of Europe and United States of Asia would unify the world. Although this is not yet a political reality, many large corporations already run the world as only three divisions: Americas, EMEA – Europe, Middle East and Africa - and APAC – Asia Pacific.

The timeline presented in the next chapter briefly covering Kali Yuga and then the beginning of ascending Dwapara Yuga, to the present day includes:

- Scientific and medical discoveries
- Expansion of travel and communication networks
- Political progress
- Social progress
- Economic progress
- Spiritual awakening
- Important books
- Ends of wars
- Pandemics, natural and man-made disasters
- Recent events echoing corresponding past events

A pattern emerges of rising tension in Kali Yuga institutions - monarchies, aristocracies, authoritarian regimes and their likes becoming unbearable for their subjects and being overthrown, with new institutions replacing them, more in line with Dwapara Yuga's vibrations.

Unfortunately, but perhaps inevitably it seems, it has taken the English Civil War, American Revolutionary War, American Civil War, WWI, WWII, Korea, Vietnam and the proxy conflicts of the Cold War, together with disasters and epidemics, so far, to dislodge old mindsets and practices. Yogananda predicted that Dwapara Yuga itself would not end world conflicts; rather in the short term intensify them.

India's peaceful independence, at least prior to partition, holds out hope for the future, as does South Africa's ending of Apartheid despite the ruling regime possessing nuclear weapons[13].

Since the Yugas previously descended and are now ascending again, as our perceptions sharpen, we increasingly are discovering that past civilizations had our inventions and structures and were not, as previously thought, 'primitive'.

Another sign of the advancing age is the increasing life span and rediscovery of healthy modes of exercise, living and eating. People are all becoming taller, again in line with ancient texts that speak of long-lived giants. They are also much healthier, recent centuries were racked with pandemics and life expectancy was short.

It will be interesting to see what develops in the domains of genetics and the prospect of complete availability of all knowledge, of everyone, all the time, everywhere. The lessons of the (ancient) past suggest not more and bigger metropoli and stressful societies but rather a simpler living, in harmony with nature.

Disasters and great reverses can be read as divine signals for change. In our immediate history, we are seeing the resurgence of Russia, China, India, Brazil, and Chile, Argentina and even now France as dissonant political philosophies are left behind.

After all, Darwin's survival of the fittest wasn't quite that, rather survival of those who adapt the best to the prevailing environment -- so the most free, open, democratic, meritocratic will prevail. Right now, despite recent mistakes like the Iraq peace and mistreatment of prisoners, that remains the United States of America.[14]

How can we see if the theory is reasonable?
1) That we should see an arc of history that reflects the ages, with corresponding dates, which appears well born out from 500 AD to 1700 AD and beyond

---

[13] http://www.globalsecurity.org/wmd/world/rsa/nuke.htm
[14] The recently published book "Day of Empire" by Amy Chua arguing that all known historical, unique superpowers have exhibited similar values on their ascendance.

2) That looking back in time we should see similar events reflected in the descending Dwapara Yuga and descending Kali Yuga, i.e. with 500 AD as the low point, we should see similar events reflected at 1700 AD and 700 BC. We should see the peak of man's civilization at 11500 BC.

The challenge here is the relative lack of knowledge of ancient civilizations since the pit of the dark ages brought about much destruction of documents. Similarly, the backwards-focused Taliban focused in their reign not in helping people, rather persecuting them and destroying the past.

We also know that there has been geographical change with many past cities potentially underground and underwater. The obvious example would be Atlantis, first mentioned in Plato's dialogues "Timaeus" and "Critias". In Plato's account, Atlantis, lying "beyond the pillars of Heracles", a naval power which conquered many parts of Western Europe and Africa in approximately 9400 BC. The Atlantic Ocean between the US and Europe and the Atlas Mountains in North Africa both are named in honor of the lost civilization. Recently man made underwater structures have been found off Japan at Yonaguni, which date back to at least 8000BC.

As of yet, there is no 'smoking gun'. If flight, say, was invented in 1900 AD, we should see flight around 900 BC and before. We have many ancient accounts of flying machines in the Vedas and the Bible, for example, followed by a deluge that set civilization back. Such descriptions support the argument but are no means conclusive since they also support alternative explanations.

If we look at the Yugas as consciousness, in the year 2007 AD, we have the same insight as in the year 1007 BC and should be able to find and understand remains from that period. As the ages rise, people become more and more in tune with the inner spiritual life and less and less focused on outer accomplishments so it may also be the case that there are less artifacts to be dug up from previous, higher ages, or they are in a form that we do not recognize for their real nature, for example, crystals or some other common item.

Timeline

3100BC Prehistory - Descending Treta Yuga closes

3300-3400BC First Sumerian and Egyptian writings are
the oldest known, prior to that, i.e. looking back into
fully developed Treta and Satya Yugas, we enter into
pre-history.

700BC Classical Antiquity - Descending Dwapara Yuga closes

700BC The Greek poet Heseod described the last Golden
Age of man, presided over by King Chronus of Atlantis.
Vases found in South America and identical vases
unearthed in Troy, by the archaeologist Schliemann,
bore the inscription, "From the King Chronus of
Atlantis."

400BC Birth of Siddhartha Gautama (Nepal) - Founder of
Buddhism

0 Birth of Jesus of Nazareth (Israel) - Founder of
Christianity
Christianity, Islam, Hinduism and Buddhism are the
world's four major religions. Of these, Hinduism is the
oldest, elements of which have been traced back to
5500BC. Strictly the term should be Sanatan Dharma,
literally, "eternal religion," the name given to the
body of Vedic teachings. Sanatan Dharma has come to be
called Hinduism since the time of the Greeks who
designated the people on the banks of the river Indus
as Indoos, or Hindus. The word Hindu, properly
speaking, refers only to followers of Sanatan Dharma or
Hinduism. We have Columbus to thank for the added
confusion of Indian being someone from India or a
native of the Americas. Interestingly Columbus'
mistake suggests a karmic link between the Americas and
India.
313 Constantine becomes first Christian Roman Emperor

500AD Lowest point of Descending Kali Yuga, Ascending Kali Yuga begins

This marked the fall of the Roman Empire, which itself
drew much of its culture from ancient Greece. It had
colonized as far as Britannia (England) and Gaul
(France). Its legacy was a model of administration and
from Latin we have Italian, French, Spanish, Portuguese
and Rumanian. The Persian Empire fell shortly
thereafter, neither being able to withstand the lows of
Kali Yuga consciousness.

529 Saint Benedict (Italy) - sets down his rules for monastic life
Monasticism was to remain almost the only spark of European culture for the next 1000 years. When the Renaissance came it drew heavily from previous more advanced civilizations in Rome, Greece and the Moslem Middle East and, as it advanced, upon the knowledge of India. Even Benedict's rule was revised over time whereby we have monasteries throughout Europe inventing alcoholic beverages such as beers, wines and champagne. The original rule had called for abstinence.
535 Climate changes dramatically - little sunshine, snow in summer. It is speculated that ash from Volcano Krakatoa had caused a volcanic winter, an echo of the 1600 BC eruption of Volcano Thera, often tied to the Old Testament stories of the Plagues of Egypt.
541 The Plague of Justinian (Italy) - thought to be the first case of plague

570 Birth of Muhammad (Saudi Arabia) - Founder of Islam

600 Stirrups (Sweden)
Allowed horses to be used in battle, changing nature of warfare

790 Viking age (Britannia) begins
Scandinavians raid then colonize British Isles, Western Europe and beyond. The scope of travel enabled by the longboat defined the Vikings. It could traverse the Atlantic, coastal waters, rivers and even be dragged over land.

1066 Norman Conquest (Britannia)
Vikings from Normandy, France take over the British Isles - the system of geographically dispersed holdings of the Normans in Britain led to cohesive nobility and a rise of the English language.

1119 Knights Templar (Jerusalem)
Establish first international banking organization

1200-1600 The Renaissance - literally rebirth

1215 Signing of Magna Carta (England)
This sets the first limit on the power of the King of England. Kali Yuga governance is characterized by brutal force, torture and oppression, seen only in modern times in the aftermath of the French Revolution and National Socialist and Communist Socialist

movements. It survives in backward pockets of the world such as North Korea, Columbia and some African states.
1229 Inquisition Formed (France) - goal of suppressing reform movements within the Catholic Church, in particular Catharism and Waldensians
1248 Gunpowder arrives in Europe (UK) - although many antecedents in China, India and Moslem world
1299 Travels of Marco Polo - first account of Europeans voyaging to the East
We still have Columbus' copy with hand-written notes. Polo's voyages, although mocked for supposed exaggeration at the time, drove the popular wish to explore the East.

1315 Great famine kills millions
1340 Black Death - total number of deaths worldwide from the plague pandemic is estimated at 75 million people, there was an estimated 20 million deaths in Europe alone

1400 Perspective in painting rediscovered (Italy)
The Greeks had it as late as 500BC since we know they used it in the painted backdrops of plays
1400 First clock towers are erected (Italy) - both Egyptians and Romans had these, using other principles and possessing greater accuracy
The regulation of time became increasingly important in industrialization, with bells and early starts used to condition whole populations in schools in North America and Western Europe for factory work.
1450 First printing press (Germany)
1453 Byzantine Empire Falls (Constantinople) - drives Italian Renaissance, taking up knowledge from Arabic world and Greece
1469 Birth of Guru Nanak (Pakistan) - Founder of Sikhism
Sikhism emphasizes equality of men, women and all castes, a sharp break with Islam and Hinduism.
1474 First patent (Italy)
1492 Columbus discovers New World, beginning of so-called Columbian Exchange (Spain)

1500 Modern musical notation developed, capable of capturing all the elements of music
Isidore of Seville, writing in the early 7th century, famously remarked that it was impossible to notate music. The record shows the capability slowly developed over the next 800 years. It was, however, possessed by

the ancients as early as 2000BC according to archeologists.

1500 Tobacco smoking introduced to the Old World
Trade in spices, tobacco, sugar, tea; coffee, chocolate, alcohol and more recently illegal drugs were early forces of globalization. In the early 90s traces of both Cocaine and Tobacco were found in Egyptian mummies dating back to before 1000BC, suggesting such trading with the New and Old Worlds had taken place in the last descending Dwapara Yuga.

1501 Typhus pandemic

1513 The Prince (Italy) Nicolo Machiavelli (1469-1527)

1516 Utopia - Thomas Moore (UK) - originally titled 'A New Atlantis'
Man begins to wake up to the possibilities of a better world and denounces some of the glaring oppressions of the time, for example, taking away common land to make sheep pasture -- forcing peasants to starvation where previously they could live free and later forcing them into factories and terrace houses. The writings inspire the formation of the Royal Society (see later). It is only in the last 100 years that men have choice in what they might become, previously, the role one was born into was life-determining -- Prince or Pauper, explaining the great love affair of the "Little Guy" in the United States and Australia, where personal effort rather than family string-pulling are admired. Unfortunately, modern America has developed its billionaire political dynasties in recent years, the last elections posing one billionaire son of a politician on the left against the same profile on the right. Before the last elections, every French candidate from left to right was the product of wealthy families, having attended the same tiny elite university - ENA.

1517 Ninety-five theses (Germany) Martin Luther (1483-1547) - launches protest movement (Protestant) against decadence and corruption in the many layers of the Catholic Church hierarchy
Luther then translates the Latin Bible into German - making it accessible to ordinary people, as much a political as a religious act (Germany)

1533 Statute of Restraint in Appeals (England) - England rejects the Pope
The Protestant idea of individual responsibility e.g. if you are poor, it is not your lot in life, rather you must personally work to improve, builds striving societies in England, Germany, Switzerland the Netherlands and Scandinavia, contrasting with the

economic sliding of Catholic Europe and the Moslem
nations where an attitude of 'it is God's will'...and I
personally do nothing. The period saw the fall of
Muslim empires, Spain and Portugal. France revived only
when the Corsican Napoleon placed an emphasis on
meritocracy. The contrast is still present between
North and South America today.
1543 Beginning of the Scientific Revolution
1543 On the revolutions of the heavenly spheres
(Poland) Nicholaus Copernicus (1473-1543)
1550 De Subtilitate (Italy) Girolamo Cardano (1501-
1576) distinguishes between electricity and magnetism
1569 Mercator Projection (Belgium) facilitates
navigation
1586 Shakespeare plays characterizes move from Middle
to Modern English (UK)
1590 First smoking ban (Italy)
In England and France beer and wine respectively were
drunk because water was usually contaminated. Low
quality foods, cigarettes, alcohol and many
prescription and illegal drugs cloud the mind, as the
ancients of higher ages knew. Amusingly in modern
times, the world's number one exporter of wine, France,
wrote a scientific paper praising the medical qualities
of wine. It was rejected by the scientific community as
completely flawed, yet it is very often quoted by wine
drinkers.
1590 European famine

1600 Ascending Kali Yuga closes with a 100-year Sandhi

1600-1700 Age of reason
Sri Yukteswar specifically mentions Gilbert, Kepler,
Galileo, Drebbel, Newton, Savery and Gray in this
period.
1602 First stocks and bonds, Amsterdam Stock Exchange
1600 Foundation of British East India Company (UK)
1600 William Gilbert discovers magnetic and electrical
effects (UK)
 (Netherlands)
1602 Foundation of Dutch East India Company
(Netherlands)
1609 Kepler discovers important laws of astronomy
(Austria)
1609 Galileo invents the telescope (Italy)
1610 Flintlock Rifle (France) - defined warfare for
next 300 years
1611 King James Version of the Bible published in
English, very strongly influences the English language

1620 European Famine
1621 Drebbel invents the microscope (Holland)
1624 Cardinal-Duc de Richelieu becomes Chief Minister to the King (France)
Besides being the foil of the three musketeers, Richelieu defined the modern nation state and the first police state, with a developed network of spies and system of bureaucratic oppression (now carried out electronically). His reign gave rise to the phrase: "The pen is mightier than the sword," as oppression and coercion moved from the purely physical to the subtle. For example, in the Academy Francaise's successful efforts to complexify French, to make it a language of elites. The American Version of English had the opposite function, to make it simpler and accessible to all. For example, the average reading age for texts in the US is kept low, facilitating commerce and immigration. To this day, it is hard for a French High School graduate to write a paragraph with no faults, a task that is simple in English. As Dwapara Yuga advanced, French was left behind since it best fitted the priorities of Kings, Nobles and more recently graduates of ENA. There is a very close connection between obscurantist language and restrictive, unionized elites in medicine and law. Incomprehensible legal texts in many nations hide illegitimate use of power and exploitation by elites.
1628 On the movement of the heart and blood in animals (UK) William Harvey (1578-1657)
1643 First Public School (Massachusetts Colony) - for all children, not simply the rich and titled
1639 First modern canal (Massachusetts Colony)
We know the ancients had canals as early as 4000BC. Perhaps given their scale they are some of the simplest ancient relics to find.
1658 Quakers Founded (UK)
ASIE: The Pennsylvania Colony was alone in not being attacked by Indian tribes while the principles of pacifism were upheld. Presidents Hoover and Nixon were Quakers.
1649 Commonwealth of England (UK) - Oliver Cromwell (1599-1658)'s Republic
1660 The Grand Tour (UK) - the elite of Britain began to tour Europe to soak up culture. In the era of mass transport, the opportunity is open to all who chose to undertake it
1661 Reign of Louis XIV (France)
One of his more ingenious ways to limit the political activity of the nobility was to establish elaborate

rules for behavior and dress. The rules for dancing were especially complicated. Many of the rules of court etiquette defined one's prestige and superiority over others. As a result, the nobles were so busy mastering appropriate court etiquette, and competing for the prestige it gave, that they had no time to plot rebellions... a fantastic Dwapara Yuga way of maintaining control, much in the way of the later Masons and Greek Societies in the US colleges...elaborate ritual and little substance.

1665 Journal des savants (France), closely followed by the Philosophical Transactions of the Royal Society (UK) in the same year begins free sharing of scientific knowledge

Great minds simultaneously tune into discoveries in different locations that have often had no contact with one another. Robert Merton, a sociologist, found that 92% of cases of simultaneous discovery in the 17th century ended in dispute. The number of disputes dropped to 72% in the 18th century, 59% by the latter half of the 19th century, and 33% by the first half of the 20th century. The decline in contested claims for priority in research discoveries can be credited to the increasing acceptance of the publication of papers in modern academic journals.

1665 Great Plague of London (UK) - recurrence of Black Death

1666 Great Fire of London (UK) - city largely destroyed

1679 Habeas Corpus Act (UK) - relief from unlawful imprisonment

1680 Golden Age of Piracy - pirate ships are the floating democracies - crews vote for a captain and treasures are shared, even among freed slaves making the ships the most free places on Earth

1687 Principia: mathematical principles of natural philosophy (UK) Isaac Newton (1642 -1727) – gravitational force

1688 Lloyds Insurance (UK) - maritime insurance, founded in a coffee house

1692 Salem Witch Trials (US)

Founded on principles of freedom, the ruling elites could not enforce their religious monopoly or their particular set of social beliefs, as pressures arose on the use of land and freedom of thought. The Puritans had found England too harsh and Holland to liberal, now in the US, the divisions lead to the founding of new colonies as their grip on power waned.

0 Dwapara

1700 Ascending Dwapara Yuga begins with a 200-year Sandhi

1700-1800 Age of enlightenment

1700-1900 Agricultural Revolution (UK)

1700 Sugar becomes worth its weight in gold, driving colonization, slavery and industrialization
1700 Britain exports the idea of the lawn, driving resource consumption from labor, to machines, to seeds and pesticides throughout the word
1700 Thomas Savery uses steam engine to raise water (UK)
1720 Stephen Gray discovers the action of electricity in the human body (UK)
1730 Sextant invented (simultaneously US and UK) - replaces the ancient astrolabe for marine navigation. Newton had discovered it 30 years before but not published the paper.
1730 Beginning of Evangelical Protestant Movement (US) The Great Awakening lead people to "experience God in their own way" pulling away from ritual and ceremony of the established church. Methodism advocated reading the Bible methodically. Many new expressions of Christianity blossomed in the US, from LDS (Mormon), to Adventists, to Jehovah's Witnesses, to Unity Church.
1732 Influenza pandemic
1744 First mail order catalog (USA) - surprisingly Ben Franklin

1750-1850 Industrial Revolution (UK)

Energy and capital become the most valuable commodities.
1755 First Dictionary of the English Language (UK)
1755 Lisbon earthquake - killing between 60,000 and 100,000 people and causing a major tsunami that affected parts of Europe, North Africa and the Caribbean. Inspired passages in Voltaire's "Candide"
1756 Concrete rediscovered (UK) - concrete is found throughout the ancient world but its formulation had been lost with the Romans. The Romans and Egyptians knew how to make concrete set under water and also how to prevent its shrinking.
1775 Influenza pandemic
1761 Harrison (1693-1776) solves Longitude Problem (UK), allowing precise naval navigation
1761 First modern factory (UK)
The mills used slave labor in the US for raw cotton, mistreated their workers in Northern England and obliged Empire markets such as India to buy their

products. Slaves were freed in 1863, India was freed in 1947, with a symbol of a local cotton spinning wheel on its flag, and conditions for workers in the UK improved. William Blake famously described them as "dark satanic mills". Engels, Marx's collaborator, had detailed the factory conditions and hoped it would fuel revolution. Ironically, neither he nor Marx could explain the improvement in conditions - it did not fit their theories. When revolution came, it was in backward, agricultural Russia.

Along with the rise of factories, terrace or row housing grew, characterized by community walls, and tightly packed populations, imposing uniformity and lack of creativity. In Western Europe, the Eastern sides of cities are typically the poor areas since they were downwind of the factories. The tradition continues in the US with cheaply built, densely packed apartments. In all societies and ages, elites retreat to rural areas with homes surrounded by large areas of land, from Hollywood stars to British nobles.

1763 Watt's Steam Engine - frees factories from being located next to fast flowing water, needed to drive water wheels.

1766 Christie's Auction House founded (UK) - efficient sellers' market

1774 Chlorine (Bleach) for cleaning and disinfection isolated

1768 Encyclopedia Britannica published (UK)

1776 Literacy in State of Massachusetts at over 90%, a side effect of Puritan Religious beliefs, similarly as for Jews or Moslems, reading Holy Texts develops literacy

1776 Independence of the United States of America

1776 The wealth of nations (UK) Adam Smith (1723-1790) Smith was one torchbearer for the Scottish Enlightenment, a period of intellectual ferment in Scotland, running from approximately 1730 to 1800.

1776 Common Sense (USA) Thomas Paine (1737-1809)

1785 Charles Wilkins (1749 - 1836) makes first translation of Sanskrit to English of the Bhagavad-Gita, opening ancient Indian knowledge to the West Sanskrit, unlike more modern languages, has an aliveness to words in that their seed sounds support many layers and nuances of meaning. For example, the words cow and horse support the idea of the everyday animals and at the same time light and energy respectively. A Sanskrit text typically has a literalist sense, often taken up by European scholars suggesting a certain primitiveness and at the same time, when read with intuition, its deeper meaning emerges. The gods, different aspects of one divinity, are described as increasing man, bringing him light, pouring on him the fullness of the waters, increasing truth in him and the demons are powers of division and limitation - coverers, tearers, devourers, confiners, dualisers and obstructers. The Transcendentalists (see later) were deeply influenced by the Gita.

1785 US Dollar introduced - becoming, over time, a world currency, rivaled today only by the Euro
1786 Birth of Davy Crockett, the last words from his journal were "No time for memos now. Go ahead! Liberty and independence forever!"
1789 French Revolution (France), inspires revolution throughout South America
In the revolution, the Virgin Mary in Notre Dame Cathedral, Paris, was replaced by Lady Liberty (an embodiment of Liberty, similar to the US Statue of Liberty or the UK's Britannia), an interesting progression from the original temple of Jupiter under the Romans then the church of the Francs in 500AD. In modern, secular France, the church is as much a museum as anything else. Huge monumental structures are not necessary for individual spiritual practice under Dwapara Yuga.
1789 Declaration of Rights of Man (France) - specifically includes privacy
1789 Metric System of measurement (France) - now world standard
1789 Bill of Rights (USA)
1792 Semaphore invented (France)
1796 First Vaccinations (UK)
1798 Essay on the principle of population (UK) Thomas Malthus (1766-1834)
1799 Fourdrinier machine (France) - first modern paper machine, along with pencil and modern fountain pen, fueled the industrial revolution, incidentally reducing the importance of clerks

1800 Second Great Awakening (USA) - continuing of the evangelical movement
1800 First Battery (Italy)
1815 End of British-American War
1816 Cholera pandemic
1819 Market crash - Panic of 1819

1821 First railway (UK) - frees cities from being located on the sea, rivers or canals, as all world's major cities are
Manchester was the first industrial city, its factories driving the Industrial Revolution and then in Lowell, Massachusetts where the model was copied. It went on to become the home of the first Red Brick University - modeled on Berlin's Humboldt University, the home of Rolls Royce, the splitting of the atom and the first modern computer. Both Alan Turing and Einstein were professors at the University.
Families were split from one another, with work no longer centered on the home, this lead to many social problems. Lowell's Mills originally were staffed only with Young Yankee women and when they were not sufficiently exploitable, by immigrants.
Interestingly it was at the age of 7 that Sri Aurobindo was sent to Manchester to study with Mr. and Mrs. Drewett.
1822 Rosetta Stone Translated (France) - Enabled reading of Egyptian hieroglyphics from descending Dwapara Yuga

1823-1941 Bengal Renaissance (India)

1828 Birth of Lahiri Mahasaya
1829 Cholera pandemic
1830 Founding of Latter Day Saints Church (USA) in Manchester, NY
The Church was a pioneer in opening up the West and building a strong social security system for its members. The Mennonites and Amish had barn raisings; LDS (Mormon) built successful cities from nothing.
1836 Birth of Sri Ramakrishna
1836 Beginning of Transcendental Movement (USA) - championed by Emerson and Thoreau
1837 Market crash - Panic of 1837 (USA) - followed by 5-year depression
1839 First solar cell (component of solar panels)(France)
1840 First national postal system at one rate (UK)
1841 First Travel Agency (UK) - organized travel for ordinary citizens
1842 End of the first Opium War with China
Britain made up its trade-deficit with China by running Opium.
1843 First Iron Ship (UK)
1845 First commercial telegraph (UK)
1845 Rules of Rugby (UK) published

Rugby went on to become the world game of football (soccer) and the US-only game of American football. The rules were set down in this year yet the game had been played at Rugby School for 200 years prior to that. It is an embodiment of the idea of Muscular Christianity i.e. combining athleticism with Christian principles. In the US, this same movement inspired the YMCA.

1845 Irish Potato Famine

1847 Establishment of Greenwich Mean Time (UK) - now a world standard called Universal or Zulu time

1847 Influenza pandemic

1848 First modern oil well (Russia)

1849 California Gold Rush (USA)

This is the most famous of several gold rushes that took place throughout the 19th century in Argentina, Australia, Brazil, Canada, Chile, New Zealand, South Africa and the United States. They symbolize Dwapara Yuga in that anyone from anywhere could become rich and successful just by making a determined effort, whether mining or more intelligently selling services. In the past, even a lifetime of hard work was no guarantee of any positive result beyond non-starvation. Via the impetus of the rushes, immigration was driven to many new parts of the world, driving the thriving cultures that continue to this day.

1850 Public Libraries Act (UK) - Public libraries open to all, not just scholars

1851 First Red Brick University (UK) emphasizes real world skills, not simply theology

1852 Mandatory Schooling (USA, State of Massachusetts)

1852 Metropolis Water Act (UK) - Sand is used to filter drinking water in London for the first time, making it truly fit to drink. Similar filters were described in Sanskrit writings of 2000BC.

1852 Cholera pandemic

1855 Birth of Sri Yukteswar (India)

1855 Cocaine isolated (Germany)

It became the wonder drug of the end of the 19th century, driving the soda fountains of Middle America where ordering a Coca Cola was described as 'taking a shot in the arm'. Ironically it was initially used to treat alcohol and morphine addiction, products that had been known for millennia

1855 Bubonic plague pandemic

1855 First mass production of steel (UK) - simultaneously discovered in US also

1856 India completely under the control of British East India Company

1857 Influenza pandemic

1858 Birth of JC Bose (India)
1858 First transatlantic telegraph cable
1858 The Great Stink (UK) - the sewage problem of
London became unbearable leading to the construction of
a modern sewage system
To this day, the modern cities of Europe are riddled
with catacombs, charnel houses and mass graves filled
to capacity with the corpses from the numerous plagues
and pestilences of the polluted cities. Paris has a
population of 2 million and catacombs containing 6
million bodies. Even as late as the Roman period, the
importance of fresh drinking water, sewage collection
and bathing had been understood. With Christianity came
an end to the old practice of burning corpses and
public bathing. Only in the mid 19th century did the
world's great cities begin building fresh water, sewage
and modern sanitation systems, the lack of which still
hold back the Third World countries.
1859 Origin of species by means of natural selection
(UK) Charles Darwin (1809 - 1882)
1860 End of second Opium War between Britain and China
1861 Lahiri Mahasaya meets Babaji (India)
1861 Birth of Rabindranath Tagore (India)
1863 Birth of Swami Vivekananda (India)
1863 Emancipation Proclamation (USA)
1863 Adventist Church Founded (USA)
The church members are to this day the healthiest
population in the US, followed by LDS (Mormon).
Cornflakes were invented to meet part of their dietary
needs.
1863 Cholera pandemic
1863 Jules Verne writes "Paris in the Twentieth
Century" which accurately predicts the pace, technology
and heartlessness of modern cities and living. It was
suppressed and only published 125 years later.
1865 End of American Civil War
1865 Assassination of President Lincoln
1864 James Clerk Maxwell (1839 - 1879) shows unity of
electricity and magnetism - electromagnetism
1866 Dynamite invented (Sweden)
1869 Birth of Gandhi (India)
1869 Market crash - Black Friday - brought about by
gold speculation
1869 Suez Canal Reopens (Egypt) - Archeological
evidence suggests it was open as early as 1878 BC
1869 Transcontinental Railroad (US) - golden spike
driven in Utah
1870 Dewey Decimal Classification of Books invented -
now used by more than 200,000 libraries worldwide

1872 Birth of Swami Aurobindo (India)
1872 Jehovah's Witness Church founded (USA)
President Eisenhower was a Jehovah's Witness.
1872 First National Park Established (USA)
1873 Market crash - Panic of 1873, initiated the Long
Depression in the United States and much of Europe
1874 Heroin synthesized (UK)
Like cocaine before it, it was initially present in
many common remedies like cough syrup

1885 First Automobile (Germany)
1886 Panchanan Bhattacharya founds The Aryya Mission
Institution
(Chief Disciple of Lahiri Mahasaya)
1877 First record player (USA)
1887 First commercial telephone (USA)
1889 Unity Church formed (USA)
1889 Influenza pandemic
1890 First athletic shoe (trainer or sneaker) invented
by Reebok (UK)
1892 Ellis Island (USA) opens to process 12 million
immigrants and Angel Island from 1910, 175,000 in the
West.
The mixture of all races and creeds in the US prevails
over the racist 'master races' touted in the West in
books such as " The Myth of the 20th Century"
1892 Birth of James Lynn (Rajarsi Janakananda,
Yogananda's most advanced disciple)
1893 Birth of Mukunda Ghosh (Parmhansa Yogananda)
1893 Birth of Minnott Lewis (Yogananda's first US
disciple)
1893 Birth of Oliver Black (Yogacharya Black,
Yogananda's second most advanced disciple)
1893 Swami Vivekananda arrives in USA
The Chicago Parliament of World Religions awakened
interest in India in the West and revivified Hinduism
in India. This marked the first formal gathering of
representatives of Eastern and Western spiritual
traditions. Today it is recognized as the occasion of
the birth of formal interreligious dialogue worldwide.
The eloquence of Swami Vivekananda (student of Sri
Ramakrishna) and his introduction of Hindu thought to
the United States are particularly remembered. The
speech has been identified by many to mark the
beginning of western interest in Hinduism. His opening
line, "Sisters and Brothers of America..." was greeted
by a three minute standing ovation from the audience.
1893 Sears Catalog (USA) - order goods anywhere, by
mail

1894 Swami Sri Yukteswar meets Babaji (India)

1894 The Holy Science (India) Swami Sri Yukteswar (1855 - 1936)

We began to hear more and more of the concept of energy in mass media. From the sixties, we begin to hear more and more of energy linked to the breath and spinal column, as esoteric truths hidden in texts and practices of religions such as Christianity, Judaism, Islam and Hinduism move from mystery schools into more public

1894 First Radio Receiver (India) - JC Bose (1858 - 1937)

Bengal, India at this time produced a wealth of geniuses from Swami Sri Yukteswar, to JC Bose, to Paramhansa Yogananda, to Sri Ramakrishna Paramhansa to Swami Vivekananda, to Sri Aurobindo, to the entire Tagore family. They all influenced both the East and the West.

1895 Birth of Basu Kumar Bagchi (Swami Dhirananda)

1896 First movie theater (USA)

1896 Birth of Manamohan Mazumder (Swami Satyananda)

Yogananda's mission began with a team of three Swamis, himself, Satyananda and Dhirananda, the latter left the path, carrying out brain research in academia.

1896 Revival of the Olympic Games (Greece)

"The sportive, knightly battle awakens the best human characteristics. It does not separate, but unites the combatants in understanding and respect. It also helps to connect the countries in the spirit of peace. That's why the Olympic Flame should never die." - 1936 Games, Hitler's speech

1897 First fingerprint bureau opens (India)

1899 Cholera pandemic

200 Dwapara

1900 Complete expression of Dwapara Yuga

1901 Marconi radios from England to Canada

1901 Nobel Prize begins -- energy of smokeless gunpowder and dynamite transmuted into force for cultural good (Sweden)

1901 Freud's works are published (Austria)

Reflections of an early addict are widely read. His student Jung came to consider the science of yoga a better path for mankind than Freud's obsessions, drawn from drug-induced dreams

1904 Geographical pivot of history (UK) John Halford, 1861-1947

1905 Special theory of relativity (Switzerland) Albert
Einstein (1879 - 1955) - shows unity of energy and
matter
1906 Food and Drug Administration Formed (USA) --
Freedom from quack medicines and adulterated foods
1906 San Francisco Earthquake - killed approximately
3,000 people, most devastating earthquake in California
and U.S. history.

1911 Beginning of Greatest Generation (participants in
WWII)
1911 Principles of Scientific Management (USA) - Taylor
- Sets out principles of mass production
1914 Opening of the Panama Canal (Panama)
1917 Tesla builds first Radar (USA)
1918 Close of WWI inspires decolonization movements
throughout the world
1918 Avian flu/Spanish flu pandemic kills twice as many
as WWI itself
1918 Beginning of movement to modern corporate
structures
1919 Formation of League of Nations (Paris)

1920 Swami Yogananda arrives in USA
In the 1920s and 30s he was the most popular speaker in
the US
1920 First commercial radio (USA)
1920 Prohibition of alcohol era begins (USA) - echoes
similar moves in Nordic countries and USSR
1920 All groups allowed to vote in elections (USA)
1921 Zenith of English-speaking British Empire, 25% of
the world (England)
1922 Yogananda establishes first ashram in the US in
Waltham "Watch City", MA
1927 Lindbergh crosses the Atlantic (USA)
Lindbergh ushered in the modern aviation era and became
the first international star.
1928 Birth of Che Guevara (Argentina)
Che came frame wealthy Irish-Argentinean stock, leaving
his original studies of medicine to help the poor. He
was ultimately betrayed by Castro, who chose power over
any campaign promises to actually help the poor on his
island, or elsewhere.
1929 Swami Dhirananda betrays Yogananda and leaves the
Ashram
1929 Wall Street Crash - Speculators trigger a
worldwide depression (USA)

1930 Dust Bowl (USA) - early ecological disaster
empties plains of farmers
1931 Birth of Osho Rajneesh (India)
1932 Famine in USSR - Communist Collectivization
starves 6 to 8 million citizens
1932 First autobahn (Germany)
1932 First Football (Soccer) World cup - A rare
highlight in this dark decade
The world becomes more and more networked -- first via
the oceans and rivers, then canals, streets, railways,
mail/courier, electricity, water/sewage,
telephone/telegraph, motorways, airports, radio,
television, cable, satellite then high speed modems. In
regimes such as France, the WWII generation of
politicians remained focused on industrial age networks
like rail and roads and their voting workers,
neglecting the importance of high speed internet in a
Dwapara Yuga economy. The present generation of the
brightest young French professionals live and work in
Britain, Switzerland or the US, a mirror of the brain
drain the UK had a generation before when its Socialist
ideologues punished success and believed the twin poles
of life were factories and public (aka council or
project) housing. Ironically, the elites of all such
utopias choose not to live the model themselves.
1932 Brave New World (USA)
Huxley embodied many of the aspects of Dwapara Yuga,
his dystopain vision, along with his one-time pupil
Orwell's '1984', warned generations of the Kali Yuga
forces which threaten to constrict society. His early
use of psychedelic drugs was taken up by official US
government programs in the late fifties and sixties in
San Francisco and Boston with the explicit aim of kick-
starting creativity. Huxley was influenced by the
Indian mystic Krishnamurti, along with other US figures
as diverse as Bruce Lee and Joseph Campbell.
1939 Sri Nerode betrays Yogananda and leaves the ashram
1939 Hewlett-Packard formed (USA)
HP was formed in a garage, starting a Silicon Valley
tradition, historically placing an emphasis on
creative, high quality products. Its biggest innovation
was social, in sharp contrast to rigid, formal East
Coast companies (IBM company "song book", Unilever's
interviewing of the entire family, not just the
candidate); it effectively invented the modern,
informal work environment. In the period where it truly
applied its own "HP Way", it was highly successful.

1940 Birth of Bruce Lee (USA)

Bruce Lee's own mixed racial heritage and openness to training students of all nationalities became a symbol of integration.
1941 First commercial television (USA)
1942 V2 weapon (Germany) - world's first ballistic missile - the same team developed both the American and Soviet missile and space programs
1942 Formation of OSS
Warfare increasingly is characterized by use of intelligence agencies, propaganda and Special Forces, for limited engagements i.e. "the few and the bright", rather than conventional armies of "the many and the dumb". The same tactics are adopted by all sides in WWII, the Cold War and now the "War on Terror." Rank in the CIA, KGB or any of the world alphabet soup of agencies becomes a path to political and economic power.
1945 Fall of National Socialism (Germany)
1945 Atomic bomb (Japan)
1945 Close of WWII and acceleration of decolonialization
Knowledge alone is not sufficient; rather it is what we do with it. Hitler kept Machiavelli's "The Prince" by his bed. Himmler kept the "Bhagavad-Gita" by his. Both had been obsessed with the past, past lives and especially India. The US General Patton frequently commented that he was reliving past lives as he fought through Europe and North Africa.
1945 British Empire wanes, American sphere of influence blossoms
1945 Formation of United Nations (USA)
1945 English emerges as world's Lingua Franca - a universal, standard language, with largest vocabulary and largest storehouse of knowledge in book form
One of the great tragedies of Kali Yuga was that in higher ages, people had perfect recall of information and had no need of books. As the ages descended, books were written down yet the great majorities were destroyed in the depths of Kali Yuga, for example, in the burning of the library of Alexandria. It is a striking fact that those that survive, from the Vedas, to the Old Testament, to the Iliad and Odyssey, to the Epic of Gilgamesh, to the Rubiyat have either an overt or a hidden spiritual message. They also tend to provide a consistent picture of past ages in which men were far from limited.
1945 Formation of International Air Transport Association (IATA)(Cuba) - organizes world air travel
1945 Birth of Bob Marley (Jamaica)

Bob was to become an important symbol of unification in the 1970s with his music - "I don't have prejudice against myself. My father was a white and my mother was black. Them call me half-caste or whatever. Me don't dip on nobody's side. Me don't dip on the black man's side nor the white man's side. Me dip on God's side, the one who create me and cause me to come from black and white."

1946 "Autobiography of a Yogi" (USA) Paramhansa Yogananda

1946 Beginning of the Baby Boom Generation

1946 Foundation of the first international business school (USA)

1947 Independence of India and Pakistan

1947 UN conference at Bretton Woods (USA) - set up International Monetary Fund, International Bank and General Agreement on Tariffs and Trade (GATT)(later WTO)

1947 AK47 Assault Rifle (USSR) - empowers the individual soldier with the firepower of a squad

1947 First sighting of a "Flying Saucer" - Washington State (USA)

1947 Alleged recovery of first UFO - Roswell (USA)

1947 First Holograph (Hungary)

1947 First Transistor (USA)

1947 Marshall Plan (USA) -- helps all the nations of Europe recover, including Germany, a stark contrast with the flawed Treaty of Versailles of 1919, which ensured another war

1948 Foundation of (modern) state of Israel

1948 UN Universal Declaration of Human Rights (Paris)

1948 Assassination of Gandhi

1948 First modern computer - Manchester "Baby" (UK) - previous WWII machines were specialist code-cracking devices

1949 "1984" George Orwell (UK)

Orwell's book highlights control mechanisms of Kali Yuga states -- Newspeak/Doublethink -- "war is peace, freedom is slavery, ignorance is strength", control of language and media, fetishistic need for surveillance and distinctions of inner party members, outer party members and disenfranchised populaces -- proles. The information age brings more and better tools for oppression yet paradoxically those same tools feed the march of freedom, liberty and democracy since satellite feeds and the Internet cannot be completely blocked by regimes in North Korea, China and France, although all three have tried hard to do so. President Chirac wanted

a French Google and French CNN, so his views and not Washington's could be imposed. It has been argued that all media reflect the interests of their owners. Thus, state owned media reflect the agenda of the regime and its owners, corporately owned media reflect the agenda of corporations and their owners. Interestingly the dual nature of the Internet to both reading and writing has only recently been harnessed by blog technology.
1949 First commercial photocopier (USA)

1949- Information Revolution (USA)

Great fortunes used to be based in agricultural land, for example, the Kings and Ministers of France then in great factories then railway, telephone, oil and commodity barons of all shapes. Today's richest man, Bill Gates, invented nothing, merely recognizing the value of other peoples' ideas and inventions from DOS to Word to VMS.

1950 Project Echelon (USA) - first steps to worldwide electronic surveillance - Big Brother is watching!
1950 First CNC (computer numerical control) machines - allow physical objects to be created from computer blueprints from wood, metal etc. blanks
1951 Original publication date for Yogananda's Gita Commentaries -- SRF Inc. suppressed them for 50 years.
1951 First video game (UK) - Checkers on Manchester Mark I
Today's video game market is larger than Hollywood.
1952 Death of Yogananda, Rajarsi Janakananda (James Lynn) becomes president of SRF Inc.
1952 Siddhartha (US) - Herman Hesse wrote the novel in German in 1922 but the US version of 1952 became hugely influential
1953 End of Korean War, following America's threat to use nuclear weapons
1953 Structure of DNA understood (UK)
1954 Beginning of Ed Parker's American Kenpo Karate (USA)
This Hawaiian LDS (Mormon) member synthesized elements of Japanese and Chinese martial arts into a uniquely American form. He discovered Bruce Lee and had many famous students, including Elvis Presley. Presley, incidentally, was influenced by Yogananda, embodying Dwapara Yuga change in bringing African American music to mainstream white audiences, in much the same way as the Beatles, Stones and Zeppelin were to follow in the 60s, also becoming involved in Eastern knowledge.

1955 Death of Rajarsi Janakananda, Daya Mata (Faye Wright) becomes president of SRF Inc.
1956 First European Song Contest (Switzerland)
1956 First Commercial Robot (USA)
1956 First commercial nuclear plant (UK)
1956 Suez Crisis (Egypt) - Britain and France attempt to maintain control of the canal and in failing, underline their now diminished diplomatic and military powers
1957 Formation of United States of Europe (Italy)
The European Community began with 6 members and is 27 now in 2007, a similar rise from the US's 13 original colonies to 50 states today. With NAFTA, the United States of Americas includes the 50 states, Canada, Mexico and practically Chile, all in line with Yogananda's predictions
1957 Sputnik Satellite (USSR)
One of the few Soviet successes, it paradoxically triggers the huge investment in technology in the West that eventually will lead to the downfall of the Socialist Communist system. Apart from narrow military and scientific bands, the Communist and National Socialist regimes had almost no cultural output (excluding those who fled them). Their propaganda models were, however, widely copied in the West, defining public opinion and driving consumer culture.
In contrast, the San Francisco of the 60s lead to military, scientific, business and artistic excellence, to the extent that the achievements of that period have not been repeatable, a triumph not of the will but real freedom and liberty.
1958 Beginning of Beat Generation (First modern subculture)
1958 Visa card launched (USA) - first true credit card
1958 Fair and Isaacs build first credit scores - enabling lending to anyone creditworthy rather than those already wealthy, or known to bankers
1958 Great Leap forward of Chinese Communists causes a famine which kills 30 million within 3 years
1959 Robert Zimmerman begins to introduce himself as Bob Dylan and a music that encapsulated an age was born (USA)
1959 Idea of the Knowledge Worker - Peter Drucker - one who works primarily with information or one who develops and uses knowledge in the workplace

1960 Beginning of Counterculture/Hippie/Psychedelics/Back To Land/Commune Movements (USA)

1960 First Laser (USA)
1960 Introduction of 800 numbers (USA) -- order goods anywhere rapidly
1960 Contraceptive Pill Introduced (USA)
1960 Great Chilean Earthquake (1960) - Biggest earthquake ever recorded, 9.5 on Moment magnitude scale, and generated tsunamis throughout the Pacific Ocean
1961 Eisenhower warns of the dangers of the Military-Industrial Complex (USA)
1961 Berlin Wall built (Germany)
Like many walls before it, from Hadrian's Wall, to Offa's Dyke, to the Great Wall of China, to the Maginot Line, it represented military and diplomatic weakness
1962 Missile escalation in Cuba and Turkey almost leads to WWIII (Cuba)
1962 Silent Spring (USA) by Rachel Carson - launches environmental movement
1963 Assassination of JFK
1963 Beginning of Generation X
1963 Equal compensation for women act (USA)
1963 First Lear Business Jet (USA) - ancestor of today's VLJs
Much as the computer, jets follow the arc of innovation from military technology, to governments, large corporations, and smaller corporations, to wealthy individuals, to the public. With the European Union it has been argued that cheap jet carriers brought real union where 50 years of bureaucracy had only brought resentment and resistance. Examples of historical planes are Rama's Pashpak and Elijah's Chariot of Fire, although those may simply be references to ascending consciousness rather than physical machines.
1964 DEC PDP8 Minicomputer (USA)
1964 Civil Rights act (USA)
1964 First facial recognition software (USA)
1965 Assassination of Malcolm X (USA)
1966 First commercial fax machine (USA)
1966 First commercial satellite (USA)
1966 First container ship (USA)
1966 Freedom of information act (USA)
1966 International Standard Book Number - ISBN (UK)
Contributes to universal access to information - trend tied to libraries, English language standard, search and retrieval systems
1966 Star Trek (USA) - essentially a utopian, Dwapara vision, drawing audiences together around the world. It covered controversial themes such as war, peace, authoritarianism, imperialism, class warfare, racism,

human rights, sexism and feminism. Most famously, the role of technology was explored, inspiring cell phones, sliding doors and research into replicators (see CNC), matter transporters and faster than light warp drives.

1967 Controversial meetings of Beatles/Stones and Maharishi (India)

1967 Sergeant Peppers (UK) - included images of Sri Yukteswar and Paramhansa Yogananda

1968 Glashow, Salam and Weinberg - unity of electroweak and electromagnetic forces

1968 Assassination of MLK

1968 Assassination of RFK

1968 International Baccalaureate (Switzerland) - a non-profit, originally to facilitate the international mobility of children of diplomats, it now provides a curriculum for students of all kinds, all ages and in all countries - a world education

1968 Whole Earth Catalog (USA) - to provide education and "access to tools" in order that the reader could "find his own inspiration, shape his own environment, and share his adventure with whoever is interested."

1968 First acoustic coupler modem (USA)

Within one generation speeds climbed from 300 baud to 3.5 Mbit/s, i.e. from a page of simple text downloading in a minute, to an entire DVD downloading in a minute

1968 Manson becomes first of many false gurus (USA)

1969 Moon landing (USA)

1969 Open University (UK) - Distance university education

1969 Led Zeppelin's Indian-Raga influenced music takes the world by storm (UK)

1969 Woodstock and Altamonte Rock Festivals (USA)

1970 Beginning of telecommuting (US)

1970 First 'No fault' divorce procedures (USA)

1970 First face lifts (USA)

1970 Standard Model of particle physics unifies all but gravity of the four fundamental forces - strong, electromagnetic, electroweak and gravity

1970 Suspicious death of Janis Joplin, Age 27 (USA)

1970 Suspicious death of Jimi Hendrix, Age 27 (UK)

1971 Suspicious death of Jim Morrison, Age 27 (France)

Compare this cluster with the births in 1892-93

1971 First laser printer (USA)

1971 Formation of FedEx (USA)

1971 First commercial microprocessors (USA)

1971 First Mars Landing (USSR)

1972 First pocket scientific calculator (USA)

1972 First UN conference on human environment (Sweden)

1972 Nixon warms world relations with China with an official visit

1973 SWIFT network for international money transfers

1973 Black-Scholes model forms basis for explosion of derivatives trading (USA)

1973 9/11 (Chile) Communist Socialistic forces are halted at the Moneda

1973 First Oil Crisis (US) -- first warning US too dependent on fossil fuels

1973 Enter the Dragon (US) - Bruce Lee demonstrates a physical unity of the East and West, absorbing the best elements from both in this masterpiece. In doing so, he became the first Asian superstar.

1973 Suspicious death of Bruce Lee (Hong Kong) - much as in the legacy of Krishnamurti, Lee's name is used and abused by many associates, perhaps his greatest legacy is the example of how anyone can become better and better to an almost superhuman extent

1975 End of Vietnam War

1975 Russia and America collaborate on Apollo-Soyuz space mission

1975 Punk movement begins promisingly with ideas of creativity a la Kabuki but rapidly degenerates into a nihilistic movement, the opposite of hippiedom, morphing into negative movements of Goths and other genres, characterized by a mindset of suicide and despair

1975 Beginning of downsizing, outsourcing, rightsizing and off shoring

Globalization drives specialization into tertiary - services, secondary - manufacturing and primary - resource extraction economies.

1977 Apple II personal computer (USA)

The PC was a culmination of size reduction and power increases from the 50s mainframes to the 70s minicomputers, placing the means of consumption and production of all media in the hands of individuals, allowing everything from animation, book production, music production, film production, architectural design, DNA sequencing to advanced simulations in the home, where previously only governments and companies held the capabilities. Combined with the Internet, it provides the resources of a Harvard or MIT in the hands of individuals.

1977 Star Wars (US) - draws on themes from Vedas to age of chivalry to Nazism, of good and evil, echoing Kali vs. Dwapara struggle, to huge commercial success

1978 Advent of GUTs - grand unified theories linking all fundamental forces

1978 First GPS Satellite (USA)
1978 Beginning of Generation Y - In West, universal
access to laptops, iPods, cellphones, digital cameras
and videos, blogs, instant messages and the Internet
1978 Jonestown massacre (Guyana)
1979 Prime Minister Margaret Thatcher elected (UK) -
together with president Reagan frees the west
1979 Second oil crisis
1979 Three Mile Island Meltdown (USA)

1980 First commercial email - CompuServe (USA)
1980 First DNA Paternity Testing (USA)
In the adult US population married people became the
minority in 2006, as societal changes make it less and
less necessary for men and women to be married for
economic, sexual, paternity or religious reasons. In
contrast, the levels of cohabitation have shot up.
1980 Launch of CNN - cable network news (USA)
1980 Beginning of the privatization movement (UK)
1981 First cellphone service (Nordic countries)
1981 President Ronald Reagan elected (USA)
1981 Assassination attempt on President Reagan (USA)
1981 Assassination attempt on Pope John Paul II
1981 First cases of AIDS (USA)
1981 First retinal scans for identification (USA)
1983 Free software foundation - forerunner GNU, Linux
etc. (USA)
1984 Assassination attempt on Prime Minister Thatcher
(UK)
1984 Bhopal Disaster (India) - world's worst industrial
disaster
1985 Live Aid (UK)
1985 Fall of Rajneeshpuram (USA)
1986 Chernobyl Meltdown (Ukraine) - world's worst
nuclear disaster
1987 Black Monday market crash (UK)
1987 Stephen Hawking of Cambridge University organized
a weeklong meeting at which scientists from around the
world brought the story of gravity up to date, 300
years after Newton's publication of the Principia (UK)
1988 First Transatlantic Fiber Optic Cable (USA)
1989 US invades Panama to ensure control of the canal
1989 Close of Cold War and fall of Communist Socialism
(Germany) - symbolically the Berlin Wall falls

1991 World Wide Web Server (Switzerland)
1991 End of apartheid in South Africa
1991 End of Gulf War I (USA)
1991 First Reality TV Show (Holland)

With a proliferation of media channels, there are insufficient sport-entertainment stars to fill them. Efforts begin to manufacture them.

1992 Black Wednesday Market Crash (UK) - mismanagement of exchange rates

1992 Hurricane Andrew (US) - 2nd most destructive in US history

1993 Webcrawler (USA) - first web search engine

1993 Siege of Branch Davidians in Waco (USA)

1994 Signing of NAFTA, joining Canada, USA and Mexico - first steps towards United States of Americas, following lead of United States of Europe

1994 Launch of Amazon.com (USA) - order all media, everywhere

1995 EU Directive on Data Protection

1995 First commercial 3-D printers (USA) - create physical objects from 'thin air' using electronic blueprints. These blueprints can be sent around the Internet, so say, a new or modified part in the US can be sent to an oil rig off African Coast and be printed out in 3-dimensions and used.

1995 Netscape launched (USA)

Henry Ford unilaterally introduced the five-day week for his workers, an early example of enlightened self-interest. Similarly, McDonalds, Wal-Mart and Microsoft grew hugely by focusing on the interests of consumers and the interests of regular employees, by sharing stocks and options. In the business world, fantastic success is closely associated with companies that share both risk and reward, for example, Netscape (USA) was the first dot com to really share wealth with all employees. Sports-entertainment, hedge funds, tech and I-banks largely define where upside is shared.

1995 Ebay launched (USA) - efficient sellers market, all objects, everywhere

Pierre Omidyar of Ebay and Sergey Brin of Google are the poster children of Dwapara Yuga - young immigrants becoming billionaires in the New Economy. Bill Gates, Larry Ellison and Steve Jobs, all college dropouts, similarly illustrate the unimportance of formal diplomas such as MBAs in entrepreneurship. In many ways the 1995 Dot Com bubble echoes the 1849 Gold Rush, with an opportunity for the bright and determined to make fortunes where previously only the wealthy and well connected had seats at the table. Similar booms accompanied the introduction of telegraphs, telephones, television etc -- notice the prefix tele for far, an echo of Dwapara's tag line of 'space-annihilator' -- with entrepreneurs in the beginning then consolidated, conservative business empires over time, until the launch of the next disruptive technology.

1995 First armed, unmanned flying vehicle deployed (US)
Such a vehicle had been proposed by Tesla 100 years before and DaVinci 500 years before but the technology to build it was not yet ready. Tesla was well ahead of his time. He had proposed homes pulling electricity from the air. His ideas were overridden by Edison and Westinghouse for the greater commercial value (to them) of installing power lines and associated infrastructure.

1996 ICQ Instant Messaging (Israel)
1996 First cloned mammal (UK)
1996 North Korean Communists cause a famine that kills 3.5 million in 3 years
1997 Asian market crash
1997 World Chess Champion loses to a computer program (USA)
1998 Russian financial crash
1998 International Space Station launched
1999 Euro introduced

300 Dwapara

2000 Y2K bug proves to be hype
Y2K was the impetus that allowed India to move into the international white-collar space. India has cultivated its elites fantastically but sadly less so general education, health, infrastructure and broader industry.
2000 Bill Gates follows example of previous US industrialists in using his fortune for world good (USA)
2000 Dot Com/Telco Bubbles Burst (USA) - Telco bubble ten times larger than better-known Dot Com bubble
2001 The first space tourist launches from Russia
2001 Launch of Wikipedia.org (USA) - surpasses both Encarta and the Encyclopedia Britannica in depth and quality
2001 Launch of itunes.com (USA) - download all media, everywhere
The iPod is a Dwapara Yuga product, conceived in India, manufactured in China and marketed from the US. India has greatly benefited from the fall of the Soviet Union and its influence. Similarly, China is benefiting much more broadly from the defacto dropping of Communist Socialist ideology.
2001 9/11 (USA)
Kali Yuga elements try to roll back time to a primitive middle ages. The symbolic targets of the World Trade

Poor Richard

43

Center and Pentagon were hit and the White House was spared thanks to heroism of ordinary passengers on Flight 93. Ironically for such a backwards aiming organization, its name, "The Network" and propagation via the Internet and focus on symbolic media victories rather than military ones show its means to be decidedly modern. It's interesting to note the stateless nature of many of the combatants, again a modern development.

2001 Post 9/11 market crash (World)

2002 Launch of Information Awareness Office (IAO) (USA) - worldwide electronic surveillance -- Bigger Brother is watching

2002 First cases of SARS (China)

2003 China becomes the third power to have a manned space program

2003 Skype Internet telephony (Luxemburg)

2003 European heat wave kills 50,000, mainly in socialist France

2004 FDA approves implantation of RFID ID chips in humans (USA) - perhaps a 'sign of the beast' for literalists ;)

2004 Indian Ocean Tsunami - deadliest in recorded history

2005 Human Genome Decoded (International Group and USA)

2005 Hurricane Katrina (US) - most destructive in US history

2007 AppleTV (USA) - integrates television, hifi, Internet

2007 Discovery of First Earth-like planet - Gliese 581 system (Chile)

This is a mirror of Columbus' 1492 discovery of America. Chile tends to embody the strengths of both the US and Europe and the weaknesses from its exposure to both National and Communist Socialism. It is already a defacto member of NAFTA, with bilateral agreements with Canada-US-Mexico, another step to a United States of the Americas. By 2020, Chile expects to have all students be bilingual in Spanish and English.

2007 The Schengen expansion of the European Union means there will be 37 states with no borders between them. This figure is set to expand to 42 by 2012.

Paramhansa Yogananda

East meets West

Classical Antiquity and Plato

The Greek Philosopher Plato lived around the 3rd and 4th century BC. The previous Dwapara Yuga had descended and the world was entering descending Kali Yuga. He, together with his teacher Socrates and his student Aristotle, was our bridge to the higher ages and the founder of Western Philosophy. Tara Mata writes in her book "Astrological World Cycles":

> "The famous Republic of Plato was largely inspired by Greek traditions founded on memories of the great civilization of Atlantis, and in two other books, the Timaeus and Critias, Plato gives vivid descriptions of the lost continent and its people. Other ancient Greeks wrote about Atlantis a the "blessed," "happy" or "fortunate" land, the Edenic garden of the world in a long-past Golden Age, remote even to the Greeks of Plato's time.
>
> Roman writers of the same period referred to the vast sea between Europe and America as Maris Atlantici, the Atlantic Ocean, thus indicating their belief that these waters covered the Atlantean continent. The Atlanteans are described by Plato and others as having been in possession of marvelous scientific knowledge and power. Particularly notable was their conquest of space by the use of airplanes and through television."

Sir Thomas More and Utopian Communities

Sir Thomas More in England in the early 16th century, just as ascending Kali Yuga was waning and Dwapara Yuga about to begin, wrote an account of Utopia, a mythical, ideal place, inspired by Plato's Republic. Its original title was "a New Atlantis". The book and the train of thought it inspired lead to the founding of the Royal Society that fueled the Scientific and then Industrial Revolutions.

It similarly sparked religious, economic and social movements that expressed themselves as communities[15]. Some of the most notable of these were

---

[15] The Palgrave companion to North American Utopias.

the Puritans, Shakers and Amish, which became part of the founding of the United States. Within the United States, the process did not stop, generating in-turn all-American movements such as the Adventist and LDS (Mormon) churches. As previously mentioned, the flow of history is not simply the renaming of high offices and redrawing of borders but a flow of ideas taken up to a greater or lesser extent by inspired men and women.

American Independence

In the 1730s a nexus of great men were born in the American Colonies. Men such as Ethan Allen, John Hancock, Patrick "Give me liberty or give me death" Henry, Thomas Jefferson, Paul Revere and George Washington were to become the Founding Fathers of a free, egalitarian United States of American, a country that embodied the values of Dwapara Yuga, a product of both the Age of Reason and the Age of Enlightenment, values that were also shortly to free France and the Spanish Colonies from Royal misrule.

A generation earlier, in 1706, Ben Franklin was born to prepare and make straight their path. He was not simply born at the dawn of Dwapara Yuga but epitomized it as a religious maverick, self-made man, great traveler (spending decades in France and England), successful businessman and scientist, ultimately that rarest breed of politician that acts for the people, rather than himself and his cronies.

His life is summarized in the phrase "He seized the lightning from the sky and the scepter from the hand of tyrants" that embodies the themes of understanding of subtle energies (nature of lightning that he discovered) and breaking down of barriers (rejecting the King of England and his misrule) that characterize Dwapara Yuga. The country he founded more than any other embodies the energy of Dwapara Yuga, tempering its sometime excessive materialism with Christian values and now yogic knowledge from India.

Franklin was a proponent of all religions. He prayed to "Powerful Goodness" and referred to God as the "Infinite". He was a true champion of generic religion, seen as a Catholic by Catholics, Protestant by Protestants and Quaker by Quakers.

His self-written epitaph was "The Body of B. Franklin Printer; Like the Cover of an old Book, Its Contents torn out, And stript of its Lettering and Gilding, Lies here, Food for Worms. But the Work shall not be wholly lost: For it will, as he believ'd, appear once more, In a new and more perfect Edition, Corrected and Amended By the Author." Thus his belief in reincarnation is his epitaph.

Bengal Renaissance

India up to Independence in 1947 was ruled from Britain just as the American Colonies had been up until 1776. The Indian Colonial Capital was the Eastern port city of Calcutta. It was the center of modern education, science, culture and politics. There was such as strong interplay between England and India that figures such as Sri Aurobindo and Gandhi received their higher education in England.

The period spanning the 19th century and early 20th century, beginning with the reformer Raja Ram Mohan Roy and ending with the poet Rabindranath Tagore was known as the Bengal Renaissance. A unique blend of religious and social reformers, scholars, writers, journalists and scientists combined the philosophies of the East with those of the West.

A nexus of great men were born in the period, beginning in the late 1820s with Swami Lahiri Mahasaya and Sri Ramakrishna, followed in the 1850s by Swami Sri Yukteswar and Swami Vivekananda and then in the 1890s by Paramhansa Yogananda, Swami Dhirananda and Swami Satyananda, together, in the US, with Dr. Lewis, Saint Lynn and Yogacharya Oliver Black whose destinies were closely tied to Yogananda's

Swami Lahiri Mahasaya

In 1861, Swami Lahiri Mahasaya, having being initiated by the reclusive Babaji[16], reintroduced Kriya Yoga to the world. Yogananda described Kriya Yoga as the "airplane" path to God, contrasting it with the theological "bullock cart" approach. Lahiri Mahasaya gave initiation to people from all walks of life, regardless of caste, religion, or place in the hierarchy of society. For a strict Brahmin, at that time, this was a courageous Dwapara Yuga inspired act. He had no desire to form any groups and as such, he did not ask his disciples to change their societal norms, daily duties, performance of worship or ritual, or the individual's personal feelings for God.

---

[16] Please refer to the chapter "Kriya Yoga Line of Gurus"

Sri Ramakrishna and Swami Vivekananda

Sri Ramakrishna is best known through his student Swami Vivekananda, who became an Indian national hero preaching Ramakrishna's message of the essential unity of all religions and also an end to colonial domination. He spoke at the 1893 World's Parliament of Religions in Chicago, marking the first formal gathering of representatives of Eastern and Western spiritual traditions. Today it is recognized as the occasion of the birth of formal interreligious dialog worldwide, launching interest in Sanatan Dharma in the West and revitalizing it in India.

Vivekananda's visit presaged the 1920 International Congress of Free Christians and Other Religious Liberals in Boston that introduced (then) Swami Yogananda to the West. In contrast to Vivekananda, the move to the United States was permanent for Yogananda.

Sri Yukteswar had considered making his organization, Sadhu Sabha, part of the Ramakrishna Mission but incompatibility of approach made that not possible.[17] Yogananda used to visit Sri Mahendranath Gupta or "M", author of "The Gospel of Sri Ramakrishna", daily. As a young man he carried a book of Ramakrishna's quotations in his pocket at all times, reading from it and, if with friends, quoting from it.

Yogananda was later friendly with Swami Prabhavananda, who continued the work of the Ramakrishna line in Los Angeles. His Vedanta center attracted various literary luminaries of the day. In Calcutta, visiting Yogananda's boyhood home, or Sri Yukteswar's ashram (now a private home), one will see revered photographs of both Vivekananda and Yogananda.

Swami Sri Yukteswar

Prior to writing the Holy Science, Sri Yukteswar had written a Yogic Bible commentary in French. Unfortunately his hopes of attending a conference in Paris and having his book published were dashed when the French authorities in India accepted the book and then suppressed it. The contents eventually became "the Holy Science", written in English, where it found a more appreciative audience. Per Satyananda's Autobiography, it was a visit from two German scholars that triggered much of Sri Yukteswar's wider thinking

---

[17] Swami Satyananda's biography of Sri Yukteswar.

on the applicability of his teachings. Yogananda recounts Sri Yukteswar's first meeting with Babaji in his "Autobiography of a Yogi":

> "'Oh, this fair is nothing but a chaos of noise and beggars,' I thought in disillusionment. 'I wonder if Western scientists, patiently enlarging the realms of knowledge for the practical good of mankind, are not more pleasing to God than these idlers who profess religion but concentrate on alms.'

Which leads to Babaji's response:

> "'East and West must establish a golden middle path of activity and spirituality combined,' he continued. 'India has much to learn from the West in material development; in return, India can teach the universal methods by which the West will be able to base its religious beliefs on the unshakable foundations of yogic science."

Indian Independence

In 1875 Madame Blavatsky founded the Theosophical Society in New York City, espousing essentially New Age teachings, drawn from Sanatan Dharma. At its height in the 1920s, there were 7,000 members in the USA alone. In India, the Theosophical society was closely associated with the Independence movement. The Indian National Congress was formed during one of its meetings.

Gandhi met with Madame Blavatsky in London in 1890, according to his autobiography. He declined to join the group but said the meeting led him to study his own religion. This meeting of Gandhi in the West with Indian-inspired Westerners parallels Sri Yukteswar's meeting with German Sanskrit scholars in India in the same period.

Yogananda was approached several times to lead the independence movement but declined. Sri Nerode, a close associate of Yogananda's, was followed by British Agents for several years on his spiritual lecture tours after an early association with the independence movement. Yogananda later initiated Gandhi into Kriya Yoga. A portion of Gandhi's ashes is located at the Lake Shrine in Los Angeles that Yogananda founded shortly before his death.

Kshanajanma purush

Swami Satyananda in his biography of Yogananda called Yogananda a "kshanajanma purush" - one who is born for the needs of his time. Sailendra Bejoy Dasgupta puts it similarly in his book "Paramhansa Yogananda Life Portrait and Reminiscences":

"If one deeply examines Yogananda's life from his birth to his last breath, one cannot escape concluding that he was simply an instrument operated by this unseen Hand - a willing, enthusiastic and dedicated instrument."

Yogananda, like Ben Franklin two centuries before him, epitomized his time, drawing together the movements of Eastern and Western thought into a blueprint for Dwapara Yuga. His autobiography begins:

"The characteristic features of Indian culture have long been a search for ultimate verities and the concomitant disciple-guru relationship. My own path led me to a Christlike sage [Sri Yukteswar] whose beautiful life was chiseled for the ages. He was one of the great masters who are India's sole remaining wealth. Emerging in every generation, they have bulwarked their land against the fate of Babylon and Egypt."

And ends

"Far into the night my dear friend-the first Kriya Yogi in America [Dr. Lewis]-discussed with me the need for world colonies founded on a spiritual basis. The ills attributed to an anthropomorphic abstraction called "society" may be laid more realistically at the door of Everyman. Utopia must spring in the private bosom before it can flower in civic virtue. Man is a soul, not an institution; his inner reforms alone can lend permanence to outer ones. By stress on spiritual values, self-realization, a colony exemplifying world brotherhood is empowered to send inspiring vibrations far beyond its locale.

August 15, 1945, close of Global War II! End of a world; dawn of an enigmatic Atomic Age! The hermitage residents gathered in the main hall for a prayer of thanksgiving. "Heavenly Father, may never it be again! Thy children go henceforth as brothers!" Gone was the tension of war years; our spirits purred in the sun of peace. I gazed happily at each of my American comrades. "Lord," I thought gratefully, "Thou hast given this monk a large family!""

Mission

Yogananda's was not an easy mission. He was a man of color with long hair and flowing robes arriving into a segregated and puritanical America just entering the Prohibition era. Even his organization in Washington had to have separate groups for whites and non-whites. Just as his teachers did not discriminate by caste or religion, Yogananda accepted students from all races, for example, making the Egyptian Hamid Bey his right hand man in the 20s.

The popular newspapers of the time presented Raja, Hatha and especially Tantra Yoga as "cults" and a "menace to white women" as part of a wider immigration backlash. In 1928, in Miami, Yogananda's life was threatened by a mob of "angry husbands".[18] Themes of psychology, sociology and sexuality were not directly addressed by Indian teachers until the 1970s and once again lead to angry mobs and similar accusations.

Despite these obstacles, from a rented room at the YMCA in Boston, Yogananda moved to having the ear of the most important men and women of the day with a headquarters in one of the most exclusive parts of Los Angeles.

Yogananda's mission was a spiritual work like the artistic work of Michelangelo five centuries before: too large for any one man to handle, requiring instead inspiration and direction of a large team. Just as Michelangelo perceived the form he was to release in each block of marble, Yogananda perceived the shining Gold of God hidden beneath the layers of mud and dirt within everyman.

As Michelangelo's life evolved, so did the forms that his works took, much as Yogananda's vision evolved from the speaking tours of the 20s and 30s to the ideas of World Brotherhood Colonies in the late 40s and early 50s. In both, the divine creations shine out, however, not every step of their lives is inspirational as they grew and evolved. A careful reading of the

---

[18] Fear of Yoga Article by Robert Love, Columbia School of Journalism, November/December 2006

"Autobiography of a Yogi" and some of Yoganandaji's contemporaries will show passages where the great Yogi sometimes slipped.

At the end of his life, much of Michelangelo's work was unfinished with figures half-emerged from stone, again a close parallel to Yogananda whose creative efforts at the end of his life were poured into writing so that posterity might continue with that inspiration.

Yogananda in India, along with Swamis Satyananda and Dhirananda established the Ranchi School for boys and the Yogoda Satsanga Society of India (YSS Inc.) and in the US, again with Swami Dhirananda, established the Self Realization Fellowship (SRF Inc.). The "Autobiography of a Yogi" details the following incident with American food:

"English strawberries for sale," cried an old woman, squatting in a picturesque open market place.

Master was curious about the strange little red fruits. He bought a basketful and offered it to Kanai and myself, who were near-by. I tasted one berry but spat it hastily on the ground.

"Sir, what a sour fruit! I could never like strawberries!"

My guru laughed. "Oh, you will like them-in America. At a dinner there, your hostess will serve them with sugar and cream. After she has mashed the berries with a fork, you will taste them and say: 'What delicious strawberries!' Then you will remember this day in Simla."

Sri Yukteswar's forecast vanished from my mind, but reappeared there many years later, shortly after my arrival in America. I was a dinner guest at the home of Mrs. Alice T. Hasey (Sister Yogmata) in West Somerville, Massachusetts. When a dessert of strawberries was put on the table, my hostess picked up her fork and mashed my berries, adding cream and sugar. "The fruit is rather tart; I think you will like it fixed this way," she remarked.

I took a mouthful. "What delicious strawberries!" I exclaimed. At once my guru's prediction in Simla emerged from the fathomless cave of memory. It was staggering to realize that long ago Sri Yukteswar's God-tuned mind had sensitively detected the program of karmic events wandering in the ether of futurity.

Although the Autobiography is filled with miracles, Sri Yukteswar never used his powers lightly; did this incident have a deeper portent than just taste? Was Yogananda's early death related to the many delicacies that he was offered in America? His family members and other disciples are all long-lived. When Yogananda visited India in 1935, Sri Yukteswar was especially critical that he was traveling with a "personal cook and a driver"[19]. Perhaps, like Vivekananda, it was the nature of Yogananda's US mission to be a short-lived one with food a mechanism for ill health. In his later years, Yoganandaji was barely able to walk and was sometimes carried by his disciple Norman Paulsen, as detailed in his book "Christ Consciousness".

Message to the World

Yogananda, a few months before his death, was asked these questions, as reported in the book "Journey to Self-Realization".

Perhaps you will agree, that the world is facing a crisis. What is the cause of it, and what is the remedy

"All nations have to follow the influence of the ascending and descending Yugas. The present world crisis is due to the upward climb of Dwapara Yuga; in order for the world to become better, evil must be expunged. The forces of evil will cause their own destruction, thus assuring the survival of the righteous nations. The conflict between good and evil has been going on since the dawn of history. However, as the world is moving upward through the Dwapara Yuga, the electrical or atomic age, there is greater potential not only for good, but also for destruction through the misuse of technology by those who are greedy and desire power. In keeping with the influence of Dwapara Yuga, technology is rapidly moving the general populace to higher levels of achievement.

---

[19] Paramhansa Yogananda Life Portrait and Reminiscences by Sri Sailendra Bejoy Dasgupta

However, the progress also creates a greater gap between the achievers and the non-achievers. This foments jealousies and social, economic and political troubles."

Would you like to give a message to the world?

"My brothers and sisters of the world: Please remember that God is our Father and he is One. We are all His children, and as such we should adopt constructive means to help each other become physically, mentally, financially and spiritually ideal citizens of the United States of the World. If in a community of 1000 persons each individual tries by graft, fighting and chicanery to enrich himself at the expense of others, each person will have 999 enemies; whereas if each person cooperates with the others - physically, mentally, financially and spiritually - each one will have 999 friends. If all nations helped one another through love, the whole world would live in peace with ample opportunity for promoting the well being of all. [...]

When every soul will rise above petty divisions in true spiritual understanding, world misery will be consumed by the fire of realization of the universality of God and the brotherhood of man. Such media as radio and television and air travel have brought us all together as never before. We must learn that it can no longer be Asia for Asiatics, Europe for Europeans and America for Americans, and so on, but a United States of the World under God, in which every human being can be an ideal citizen of the globe with every opportunity for fulfillment in body, mind and soul. That would be my message, my plea, to the world."

Art of living

Yogananda wrote the following paragraphs in the East West Magazine of May 1933. They are, in the author's opinion, one of the most succinct summaries of his teachings.

"Every man builds his aspirations and forms his desires according to his pre-natal and post-natal influences. Heredity and national, social, and family characteristics, tastes, and habits mold the life of a child. Children, in the beginning of their lives, are about the same everywhere. That is why Jesus said: "Suffer little children to come unto me, and forbid them not, for of such is the Kingdom of Heaven." Divinity is the one nationality of all children the world over, but, as they grow older and the family and social characteristics begin to exercise their influence, it is then that individuals begin to reveal the Hindu or American or any other national and racial traits.

It seems as if God is trying to evolve the art of right living by expressing His Truth through a combination of particular civilizations, mentalities, and nationalities. No nation is complete in itself. An absorption and collection of the best in Hindus, English, Americans, Chinese, French, German, and other nationalities may offer us the best information on the art of living. It is important to note that certain individuals like Jesus, or the master minds of India, not only attained the best in all civilizations since the earliest era to the present time, but they manifested the highest ideals embodied in all religions.

Great men and saints always live several hundred years ahead of their time and exemplify the universal Truth of all times. Therefore, the art of right living can be found in the study of the best in all nationalities, plus the study of the individual lives of great saints. Of all nationalities at present, the Hindu and the American represent, respectively, the acme of spiritually and materially efficient civilizations. The Hindus and other Orientals have produced the highest types of spiritual people, like Jesus and Ghandi. Whereas, Americans have produced the greatest types of businessmen, like Henry Ford, and also practical scientists like Thomas Edison. A combination of the spiritually efficient qualities with the scientific materially efficient qualities as represented in the above examples of the lives of great men can offer us an art of living which will produce physically, mentally, morally, materially, socially, and spiritually the highest type of all-round men in all nationalities.

The next things is to select, not the particular one-sided national characteristics, but the all-round universal principles of living from all nations and from all great men. Do not take only those principles which develop the physical at the cost of the spiritual phase of man's life, or vice versa, but also take those which equally and harmoniously develop the superman with his balanced physical, mental, moral, and spiritual qualities.

I will now enumerate a few practical methods of uniformly developing body, mind, and soul.

(a) Eat more raw food and fresh fruits, drink fresh milk and plenty of orange juice with groundnuts mixed in. (Read and follow a good modern book on dietetics.[20])

(b) Fast one day a week on orange juice and use a suitable cleansing mineral oil as prescribed by your physician.

(c) Walk, run, or take some form of vigorous exercise with deep attention until you perspire, every morning and evening.

(d) Read and meditate upon a passage from the Christian Bible and a passage from the Hindu Bible, (Bhagavad Gita) obtainable at any large book store.

(e) Read Shakespeare and other classics, some portions from some practical books on chemistry, physics, physiology, and history of Oriental and Western philosophy, comparative religion, ethics, and psychology. Don't waste your time on cheap novels. Read a good health and spiritual magazine. Read the editorial and health articles in the newspapers, and not only the comics and scandals.

(f) Go to a different church each Sunday. One Sunday go to the Protestant church, another Sunday go to the Catholic Church, another Sunday go to the Jewish temple, and another Sunday go to the Hindu temple, and so on. Keep on doing this in rotation to show not only your toleration, but to develop your appreciation and understanding. Call all temples, whether Christian, Jewish, Hindu, Buddhist, or any other religion, by the common name—"The Temple of Our God."

(g) While honoring God in all man-made temples, learn to worship and contact Him in the temple of deepest silence. Practice meditation[21] for one hour in the morning and one hour at night. Learn the highest methods of scientific concentration and meditation as taught by great Hindu masters. Do not be sidetracked to dogmatic untested religious beliefs, but try to find the one highway of Self-Realization that leads quickly to God through the forests of belief and theology. Do

---

[20] The author recommends looking at "The Zone" by Dr. Sears and also "Eat right for your blood type" by Peter D'Adamo.

[21] In order to learn Yogananda's Kriya Yoga technique, refer to the chapter "Major North American Kriya Yoga Organizations".

not be a slave to the senses. Learn to make them serve you with lasting spiritual pleasures.

(h) Only occasionally go to see the best moral and spiritual plays or moving pictures.

(i) Obey the good laws of your family, country, and all nations.

(j) Speak kindly and follow fearlessly the Truth wherever you perceive it.

(k) Love your family and country deeply so that you may learn to love and serve people of all nations more, and learn to find God in all men of whatever race or religion.

(l) Earn more, and spend less by destroying luxurious habits. Save enough so that you can live on the interest of your savings. Divide your life into four parts, putting the main emphasis on developing particular efficiency in one line during each of the four periods of life.

(1) From 5 to 25 years, take up the study of efficiency, general education, and particular training;
(2) from 25 to 40 years, earn money;
(3) from 40 to 50 years, live quietly, study, and meditate;
(4) from 50 years on, spend life in preaching and meditating deeply.

In short, remember, if you think of making money for half an hour, exercise one hour, if you exercise one hour, read two hours, and if you read two hours, meditate three hours and love God and act peacefully at all times. Learn to be calmly active and actively calm.

Say this prayer: "Heavenly Father, teach us to create an United States of the World with Thy Truth as our leader and president, which will guide us to live in loving brotherhood, and urge us to develop our bodies, minds, and souls perfectly, in order that Thy Kingdom of Heavenly Peace which is within us may be manifest in the actions of our daily life."

Pray also: "Heavenly Father, may Thy love shine forever on the sanctuary of my devotion, and may I be able to awaken Thy love in all hearts. Make me efficient, healthy, perfect in everything, so that I may inspire all my earthly brothers to be Thy noble children." Above all, contact God first in the Temple of Silence, and then health, prosperity, and wisdom will be added unto you.

The aeons one by one are flying;

> The arrows one by one are gone.
> Dimly, slowly, life is fading;
> But still my soul is marching on."

Martial Arts and Sports

Yogananda's brother, Bishnu Charan Ghosh, was one of the early pioneers of Hatha Yoga and bodybuilding both in India and the West. Other than adapting Kriya Yoga for the West, Yogananda also invented the Yogoda (now known as Energization) Exercises in 1916.

Yogananda himself was extremely fit and a great athlete in his youth. Family members recount that one of his typical activities was challenging formidable Calcutta security guards to wrestling matches ... and winning. At Mount Washington, he was unbeatable on the tennis courts. A number of his early companions were met on football (soccer) and hockey fields rather than in ashrams.

His guru, Sri Yukteswar, was described thus in the biography by Swami Satyananda: "Besides pursuing the knowledge of many different subjects, he was also interested in physical culture. With his naturally athletic body, he was able to excel in sports such as horseback riding, hunting, weapons' sports etc." He believed martial arts were necessary and worthy of being part of formal education. Yogananda uses the theme in his book "the Law of Success":

> "A and B were fighting. After a long time A said to himself: "I cannot go on any longer." But B thought: "Just one more punch," and he gave it and down went A. You must be like that; give a last punch. Use the unconquerable power of will to overcome all difficulties in life."

This has the same stamp as the well-known story of Sri Yukteswar's:

> "My mother once tried to frighten me with an appalling story of a ghost in a dark chamber. I went there immediately, and expressed my disappointment at having missed the ghost. Mother never told me another horror-tale.
> Moral: Look fear in the face and it will cease to trouble you."

Swami Vivekananda had once remarked, "If you want to understand the Gita, play football!" Swami Kebalananda, Yogananda's Sanskrit tutor, was similarly an excellent athlete. Yogananda explains the importance of sports, especially martial arts at his Ranchi Boy's School in the following "Autobiography of a Yogi" passage:

"Sports and games are encouraged; the fields resound with hockey and football practice. Ranchi students often win the cup at competitive events. The outdoor gymnasium is known far and wide. Muscle recharging through will power is the Yogoda feature: mental direction of life energy to any part of the body. The boys are also taught asanas (postures), sword and lathi (stick) play, and jujitsu. The Yogoda Health Exhibitions at the Ranchi Vidyalaya have been attended by thousands."

Interestingly the English Public School Rugby, mixed Christian principles with exercise, formulating the rules of rugby and football. In the 1950s and 1960s, Ed Parker, with Kempo, and Bruce Lee, with Jeet Kune Do, similarly combined spiritual values with exercise. Historically, martial arts and spirituality had always been combined in monasteries but became split by political and criminal gangs, who needed only the physical abilities.

It is worth emphasizing that Yogananda's mission was meditation rather than the popularization of Hatha Yoga, which deals with postures and is really a preparation for meditation. Extreme body identification alone was part of the cults of National and Communist Socialism with their themes of ideal youth.

"My relationship to power and authority is that I'm all for it. People need somebody to watch over them. Ninety-five percent of the people in the world need to be told what to do and how to behave."
Arnold Schwarzenegger in a 1990 interview with U.S. News.

Sacred Places

Yogananda considered Los Angeles to be the Benares (Varanasi) of America, its most Holy Site. The reasoning was not based upon the present vibrations but those of a previous city and civilization with a much higher vibration, at the same location. Similarly, Native Americans hold many remote areas to be particularly holy. Perhaps these too had special significance in previous ages.

In the book "Discovering the Mysteries of Ancient America: Lost History And Legends, Unearthed And Explored", a large number of archeological finds are detailed showing North America to have been inhabited with sophisticated peoples for many tens of thousands of years, rather than the classical view of more recent, primitive people. Two astounding claims in the book are of the presence of Caucasian peoples and many buried tablets. Both of these would tend to confirm the assertions of the LDS (Mormon) Church.

In Europe, we see successive temple and church building on locations held as holy for thousands of years. The large numbers of such places have given rise to the idea of Ley Lines. Certain of the sites have been found to have physical differences from the surrounding areas, for example, in magnetism. Yogananda suggested another factor in that people repeatedly raising their consciousness in a particular setting over a period of time raised the vibration of the location, which suggests how certain sites could become more and more charged, particularly in higher ages when the level of consciousness was generally higher.

In Feng Shui (the Chinese art, itself derived from the more ancient Indian, Vastu Shastra) householders are specifically advised to avoid living near hospitals, mental institutions, police stations, military bases, discos, bars and other areas where vibrations tend to be low. Looking at Ascending Kali and Dwapara Yugas, there has been a definite geographic move from the Middle East, to Europe and now to North America, with certain cities in turn showing phenomenal creativity and then fading away, perhaps as their vibrations move into and out of harmony with the vibration of the Yuga. In modern India, once sleepy Bangalore (Bengalaru) has surged while previous intellectual powerhouse Calcutta (Kolkata) has faded, one embracing modern technology and the other Socialist Communism from the Kali Yuga consciousness.

Reincarnation

Paramhansa Yogananda named the following reincarnations, which would mean that the same 'actors' drive major changes in the world.

Recent World Actors:
- Charles Lindbergh was Abraham Lincoln

- Churchill was Napoleon
- Hitler was Alexander the Great
- Kaiser Wilhelm was Julius Caesar
- Mussolini was Marc Anthony
- Stalin was Genghis Khan

General Patton believed himself to be reincarnating to fight a battle previously fought (and at that time, lost) against Field Marshal Rommel. As mentioned in the timeline, Hitler and other top Nazis, held similar beliefs in reincarnation. Churchill appointed a so-called "Black Team" of occult advisers. It may be that just knowing astrological predictions given to Hitler gave the Allies the edge. In more modern times, Ronald Reagan took astrological advice and the Fascist turned Socialist President of France, Francois Mitterrand, traveled regularly to Egypt to commune with the Pyramids, believing himself linked to the past dynasties.

SRF Inc. Actors:
- Yogananda was Arjuna of the Gita, was William the Conqueror, was William Shakespeare
- Kriyananda (ex SRF Inc. Vice President) was William (the King)'s son
- Daya Mata (current SRF Inc. President) was William (the King)'s daughter
- Babaji was Krishna of the Gita, was "One of Three Wise Men" of the Bible
- Lahiri Mahasaya was King Janaka, was the poet Kabir, was "One of the Three Wise Men" of the Bible
- Sri Yukteswar was "One of Three Wise Men" of the Bible, was Saint Francis of Assisi
- Tara Mata was Leonardo da Vinci
- Rajarsi Janakananda was Nakula of the Gita
- Dr. Lewis was Sir Francis Bacon
- Therese Neumann was Mary Magdalene

Yogananda revealed to Kriyananda that everyone currently living on this planet is somehow connected from past lives and those being incarnated presently are from four main groups:
- Native Americans coming back as Environmentalists
- Atlanteans coming back to drive technology
- Romans, with their ideas of Grand Republics

- Westerners incarnating in India and conversely Indians incarnating in America

In India, the ashrams are filled with wealthy westerners with impressive degrees and family connections fleeing materialism, while Indians increasingly dominate in business in Britain, the US and around the world, leveraging the same backgrounds to reach that same materialism. The happy medium is somewhere in between and many examples of house holder saints can be found on the pages of this book, from Dr. Lewis to Saint Lynn to Yogacharya Oliver.

Environmentalism is becoming more and more of a force, especially where coupled with Atlantean Technology and Indian Yoga, a pleasant alternative to the Roman model of permanent wars, existing to pay taxes and oppressive rule.

Organizational Squabbles

Paramhansa Yogananda founded SRF Inc. and passed it to his most advanced follower, Saint Lynn, upon his death in 1952. From 1955, following Saint Lynn's death, the organization was taken over by a small group of ex-LDS women. During his lifetime, Yogananda had particularly emphasized a number of key ideas, as outlined in his "Art of living":

1) The idea of the Householder Saint who is successful spiritually, in family life and in business, as exemplified by Lahiri Mahasaya, Sri Yukteswar, Dr. Lewis, Saint Lynn and Yogacharya Oliver Black;
2) A future of families grouped together in like-minded World Brotherhood Colonies;
3) The idea of making a Christian a better Christian, a Jew a better Jew etc. rather than forming a completely new religion;
4) Practice of sport and martial arts;
5) Development of a rounded culture, especially spiritually;
6) Independent action for spiritually advanced disciples.

Instead, the organization became increasingly autocratic, placing an undue emphasis on monasticism and puritanism, heavily editing Yogananda's original works to place an accent on organizational loyalty and holding up printing of Yogananda's works such as his Gita Commentaries for decades.

To give just one example of the changes: in 1960, SRF Inc. required Kriyabans to sign a pledge renouncing all other church affiliation, and accepts exclusive membership in Self-Realization Fellowship Church, a direct contradiction of Yogananda's instructions. In one letter, this stopped Yogananda's mission in Europe for decades.

The new regime were known as the Matas since the women consisted of a number of LDS converts including Daya Mata (Faye Wright), Ananda Mata (Virginia Wright, Daya's sister), Mrinalini Mata (Merna Loy Brown) and Tara Mata (Laurie Pratt, Yogananda's editor). Daya's brother, Richard Wright, Yogananda's secretary, and her mother where also SRF Inc. members. Daya and Tara's families were important members of the LDS community. Daya's father had helped build the Salt Lake City Temple and Tara's grandfather had been Joseph Smith's editor, the same role she now held for Yogananda. Tara's family is related to Mitt Romney, the current (2007) LDS candidate for the US Presidency. Daya Mata is listed by the State of Utah as one of its most famous daughters.

The Matas systematically purged the ranks of Swamis, advanced male disciples and anyone capable of standing up to them, leaving India in the dust. For example, Swami Premananda was ordained a Swami in 1941 by Yogananda and it was he who performed the Vedic rites at Yogananda's funeral in 1952. He and his organization in Washington, DC, were airbrushed out of existence. The list of those leaving was long, including Yogananda's most advanced living disciple Yogacharya Oliver Black and the man he had personally chosen to lead his monastics: Swami Kriyananda.

In 1990 the Matas decided to silence ex Vice President of SRF Inc. Swami Kriyananda since his organization Ananda was essentially rivaling in size and public awareness the original SRF Inc. They spent several million dollars and twelve years in a lawsuit[22] that ultimately opened up the legacy of Yogananda's writings to the general public. The price Swami Kriyananda paid was character assassination by SRF's legal team. SRF's heartless tactics simply caused more monastics and members to leave, especially when the luxury lifestyle of bizarre trips to Disneyland, vintage pink Cadillac and multi-million dollar mansion[23] of Daya and her sister became better known.

---

[22] yoganandarediscovered.org press release January 3, 2003
[23] New Times Los Angeles, June 1, 2000

Dwapara Yuga and Yogananda: blueprint for a New Age

In some ways, the Matas are simply repeating the history of their own LDS Church, which splintered at each leadership succession and was forced to reform due to outside pressures. Even today, LDS's highest officers (against the founder's written wishes[24]) live in paid luxury and, just as for SRF, the lay members work without pay. The monastic aspect of the SRF Inc. organization (independent of the original teachings) is often compared to the Catholic Church. The all-male SRF Inc. Hidden Valley Retreat (established by the Matas in 1982) has similar issues, as do all-male Catholic Seminaries. Sri Yukteswar had particularly wanted to avoid this, being opposed even to the closeness of Yogananda and Dhirananda on principle, not because there was any impropriety.

SRF Inc. Archives

The Matas are very slowly releasing archival material. For example, Daya Mata's Brother Richard Wright's travel diaries and films from Yogananda's 1935 trip to India have still not been published. Yogananda's commentaries on the Gita and Bible were 50+ years in 'editing.' Many of the great men and women of the early 20th century do not figure in this book since their correspondence is being kept under lock and key.

In the 1930s Yogananda saw the menace of Communist Socialism as a movement that would take away the emphasis of individuality and inner search in favor of lock-step conformism. In the 1950s he urged for American intervention in Korea against Communist Socialist influence and against Communist Socialist Collaborators in the US.

It took great energy for Yogananda's mission. Even his most advanced disciples were not able to get much traction until the late 1960s and early 70s when popular consciousness had risen enough for movements such as back to the land to take off. The 80s and 90s saw a backlash of nihilistic youth movements such as Punk, Goth and Gangsta Rap robbing people of hope and positivity.

Interestingly in the mid to late 2000s, the American television shows "Lost" and "Heroes" draw heavily on elements of Sanatan Dharma thought and have been huge international hits, with an emphasis on hope and personal effort even in the face of crushing odds.

---

[24] "… hireling priests, whose object and aim were to keep the people in ignorance for the sake of filthy lucre; or as the prophet says, to feed themselves, not the flock."
Teachings of the Prophet Joseph Smith,

Only now with the advent of the Internet, is more information coming to light as to Yogananda's historical impact, from small things such as Norman Paulsen's beginning the Natural Foods movement in California, to Yogananda's direct influencing of the major industrialists.

Even the Vatican's Secret Archives have been opened to the public since 2000 AD so SRF Inc. is a now "more Catholic than the Pope" in its secrecy with Yogananda's archives. Yogananda said his works would bring millions to God. It seems selfish for SRF Inc. to withhold the archives; perhaps because they illustrate some of its organizational challenges and that a Guru speaks sometime inconvenient truths.

Those who went away

Yogananda was realized. In person, he didn't make people read lessons, wait and complete tests by mail. If someone was ready, he initiated him or her, or initiated him or her to initiate others. Period. He said when I am gone, the writings are the guru. A title of swami, brother, sister, light bearer means someone has made certain commitments and holds an organizational role but that should not be confused with a guaranteed degree of enlightenment, as illustrated by the following three examples.

Leslie Van Houten moved on from being a nun in SRF Inc. to joining Charles Manson's "Family" in the late 60s. Yogananda talked of two "Judases". The first was Swami Dhirananda[25], Yogananda's boyhood friend, who came over in 1922 and was number two in SRF Inc. but quit in 1929 and successfully sued Yogananda in 1935 for his share of SRF Inc. The second was Sri Nerode[26], who traveled and lectured in Yogananda's place. He quit and sued Yogananda unsuccessfully in 1939, along the same lines of Swami Dhirananda. It is instructive to look at SRF Inc. in 1933, as detailed in East-West Magazine:

Honorary Vice Presidents 1933:
- Yogi Hamid Bey[27]
- Brahmachari Nerode
- Brahmachari Jotin

---

[25] Dhirananda went on to do important research in brainwaves leading to today's devices that let computers be controlled by brain activity alone.

[26] Sri Nerode continued to teach in his own right. He is the person being married in the popular Internet video of Yogananda in which we also see Hamid Bey

[27] Founded the Coptic Fellowship in 1937

Ministers 1933:

- Sradha Devi
- Ranendra Kumar Das
- Upadeshak Punditji
- Sister Gyanamata
- Sister Bhakti
- Salome E. Marckwardt
- Mary Broomell
- Ma Durga
- Yogi F. Sevaka

Of this group, only Sister Gynamata and Ma Durga stayed. Notice that there is no special mention of Daya Mata or her sister. Organizationally especially what should be a calling is sometimes just an administrative job and the higher the role, sadly, sometimes the more administratively-minded the person, or worse, more desirous of wealth, power and fame. In fairness, every large group is almost bound to have some bad apples. Even Butch Cassidy was an LDS (Mormon) member.

In Tibetan Buddhism, the Dalai Lama is not the spiritual head, rather the political head. The present Dalai Lama's role is one of fund raising and lobbying. In the Catholic Church, spiritually advanced priests have historically always been an embarrassment rather than a boon since they rock the organizational hierarchy with its emphasis on administration. No matter how illustrious or notorious the organization, the effort to meditate is personal.

Businessmen

Yogananda's guru was a real estate investor, his paramguru an accountant and his saintly father a railway Vice President. All three were household saints, succeeding in business, family and spiritual spheres. It was the business acumen of Yogananda's father, then Dr. Lewis and finally James Lynn that funded Yogananda's mission in the West.

- Dr. Lewis (Dentist and Real Estate Investor)
- James Lynn
  (Insurance millionaire, Yogananda considered him his "Businessman Saint" and most advanced student)
- Yogacharya John Oliver Black
  (Auto parts industrialist, Yogananda considered him second most advanced student)

- Luther Burbank
  (Horticultural pioneer, Yogananda's "American Saint")
- Henry Ford (Ford Motors)
- George Eastman (Kodak)
- William Wrigley (Gum)

More recently, Vinod Dham, the architect of both the Intel and AMD chips that power today's computers is "Prone to bedside reading of the Bhagavad Gita and Yogananda's Man's Eternal Quest" [28] Thomas Edison was friends with both Henry Ford and Luther Burbank. Yogananda described Burbank and Edison as "standing in blazing flame" due to their "extraordinary quality of initiative."

Paraphrasing, Yogananda said the second most difficult thing to achieve in this world after realization was that of being a successful businessman, since the qualities of one-pointed attention and continual thought of business are so similar to what is needed to find God. Yogananda writing to Oliver Black, 1951:

> "With your organizational power you can do something much greater, much more lasting, much easier, and much more secure than present-day business organizations in which one works to pay taxes, ruining his health and happiness. Detroit, being in the center of the United States, has a great opportunity to draw true seekers, both from the East and West. I would like nothing better than for you to establish a sub-headquarters there."

Swami Kriyananda has made the link much more explicitly in his course "Material Success through Yoga Principles" [29], offered in India. It is worth pointing out that all of these disciples were married, or householders, including Norman Paulsen, Swami Kriyananda and Roy E. Davis. Of the SRF Inc. monastics, the one most mentioned in this book, Tara Mata, left SRF Inc, married and had a child, before returning to the organization.

---

[28] The Horse That Flew - by Chidanand Rajghatta
[29] http://www.materialsuccess.com/

Politicians

Yogananda was several times approached to lead the liberation of India but declined to participate, predicting the struggle would be won by non-violent means. His student Gandhi finally achieved independence in 1947.

He met privately with US President Coolidge in the 20s and corresponded with

- Dr. Binay R. Sen, Indian Ambassador to the U.S
- Emilio Portes Gil, President of Mexico
- Goodwin J. Knight, Governor of California

To this day, California remains the most advanced state in the Union and the US the most advanced country in the world. Kriyananda recounts an assassination attempt during the depression years when Yogananda reproached the rich for exploiting the poor. His great will saved him and reformed the life of the assassin, without a struggle.

As detailed in Kriyananda's "The Road Ahead", Yogananda foresaw a coming together of the United States of Americas, of Europe and of Asia and an exchange of influence between the US and India. The European Union was formed in 1957, 5 years after his death and now has 27 members, with more, such as Turkey, waiting in the wings. NAFTA was signed in 1994, bringing together the US, Canada and Mexico, with Chile now a defacto fourth member.

India is gradually casting off the evils of caste politics, corruption and Communist Socialist paymasters, becoming a first world power. Many of India's elites now live and work in the US and many US businesses have large presences in India. India is rapidly assimilating the materialism of the US and the US is assimilating the spirituality of India.

In the short term, Japan, England and France will pay for their past exploitation and colonization. England and France have lost their world power since Suez and appear to be in steady decline, with a reverse colonization in effect, members of which are increasingly the business, sport-entertainment and intellectuals of today e.g. France's new president is an immigrant and Britain's elites are dominated by Scotland, a tiny subject nation. Japan's salary man culture has burned itself out and Korea and China, once subject nations of Japan, are overtaking it.

Dwapara Yuga's revealing of subtle energies, will lead to better understanding and cures of disease and at the same time better weapons. The US and Russia are working to weaponize subtle energies, as detailed in the book "Remote Viewers".

Musicians

Musicians tend to be some of the most open and creative people in society and have phases of interest in many things and many religions, movements and groups, over their lifetimes. Musical ability is no proxy for enlightenment.

With those caveats, here are some musicians who have been associated with Yogananda:

- Amelita Galli-Curci
- Elton John
- Elvis
- George Harrison - song Dear One
- Gregg Almann
- Leopold Stokowski
- Supertramp - song Babaji
- Swami Kriyananda within SRF Inc. and Ananda but also more publicly with Derek Bell of the Chieftains
- Yes - Tales from Topographical Oceans - double album inspired by Yogananda

The LA Times in 2006 relates the following Elvis story:

"Residents of the Mount Washington complex still talk about the time in the late 1960s when Elvis Presley showed up at their door. Elvis looked at one of our monks and said, 'Man, you made the right choice,' recalled Brother Paramananda, who left a promising acting career to devote his life to the fellowship. Elvis said, 'People don't know my life or that I sometimes cry myself to sleep because I don't know God.' Fellowship leaders encouraged him to continue singing."

Many other musicians, especially in the jazz world, have been associated with other Yogis. Recently Robin Gibb of the Bee Gees launched a worldwide promotion of meditation. I believe it was Osho who observed that the poor are focused on their next meal, the middle class on career advancement and the wealthy, who have exhausted their appetites for material goods, drug and alcohol trips, sexual adventure, travel and thrills, search for spirituality.

UFOs

Kriyananda relates the following Yogananda story:

> "When Paramhansa Yogananda was once in one of his ashrams in Twenty-Nine Palms, California, he observed how one of his disciples was rather obsessed with UFO's. Now, you may be aware that there has been much UFO activity in certain desert areas of western USA since the 1940's, and probably even before that. So Yogananda, using his powerful will, decided to settle the matter with this disciple, once and for all. One evening he said to the interested party, 'Take a look out the window'. As she did so, several UFO's appeared right in front of the ashram in clear view for all to see. Yogananda then said, 'Right. You've seen them; now forget about them!'

Kriyananda makes the same point as Yogananda that meeting pilots, engineers and technicians from some fantastic flying device whether from this planet or another, although interesting, is not necessarily enlightening in the spiritual sense. Yogananda's student Norman Paulsen pursued the UFO angle strongly and an account of that research and his time with Yogananda can be read in his book "Christ Consciousness".

In 2007 a telescope in the desert of Northern Chile found the first earth-like planet. The area boasts the clearest skies, ancient drawings that can be seen only from the air, tens of US research centers and one of the most famous high energy/sacred spots in Latin America: Cochiguaz.

Blueprint for a New Age

Preparation

- 245 Dwapara - The atomic bomb was dropped in 1945.
- 246 Dwapara - The "Autobiography of a Yogi" came out in 1946.
- 266 Dwapara - 1966 was the height of the awakened hippie and back to the land era
- 286 Dwapara - 1986 egotistical yuppie generation, backlash
- 306 Dwapara - 2006 growing consciousness of natural living and striving for new models of world peace

Yoganandaji's predictions for early Dwapara Yuga were not all rosy; he foresaw a Third World War and a Great Depression, even greater than that of the 1930s, as detailed in Kriyananda's "The Road Ahead".

> "The means by which we live have outdistanced the ends for which we live. Our scientific power has outrun our spiritual power. We have guided missiles and misguided men."
> Martin Luther King

How can we prepare for these events?
- Buy land away from cities, with inexpensive taxation, yet still near a small town
- Build your own home and have the least mortgage amount possible
- Grow your own food, as far as is possible
- Stay fit
- A mainly vegetarian diet is healthy and inexpensive
- Be as self sufficient in energy as possible
- Ideally have your own well and filtration
- Stockpile food, upwards of 1 month's supply
- Consider alternative transport means
- Comply with local laws, taxes and regulations
- Have savings rather than debts
- Have investments in tangibles such as land, home, gold and silver as well as conventional paper money, stocks etc. (which can simply evaporate in a crisis)
- Leverage modern options for telecommuting and Internet businesses

The same guidelines apply for natural disasters or civil unrest. The LDS (Mormon) church also has these guidelines as official policy, given its history of persecution and hard times.

American Red Cross	redcross.org/services
DIY Emergency Preparedness (MT)	nodoom.com
General Survival (ID)	alpinesurvival.com
LDS (Mormon)	providentliving.org

Some of these ideas are familiar to those living in the Western US, given its pioneer past but may seem alien to those living on the US East Coast or in Western Europe. Living memory has seen National and Communist Socialist murder in Europe, the bloody partition of peaceful India, the Israel-Palestine conflict, death squads in South America, the ethnic cleansing and return of concentration camps in the Balkans through to today's world-wide terrorism.

If these events do not come to pass, you simply have made good investments and live in a healthy environment, if they do, you can save family, friends and more. Politicians and the wealthy have professional advisers (weathermen to know which way the wind is blowing) that have their rural and coastal compounds already prepared.

In Dwapara Yuga, knowledge of all kinds from Kriya to simple preparedness is no longer the preserve of elites. The goal is not to have disaster consciousness, rather to be prepared for what are becoming increasingly likely events, whether one lives in San Francisco, New York, London, Paris, Delhi, Santiago or Sydney.

Mass culture

Yogananda's 1933 'Art of Living' harks back to the culture of the Bible and Shakespeare. In later years he warns of the dangers of the mass culture of radio, cinema and television, which have broad reach yet often a shallow depth. Similar warnings came from Christian Ministers.

> At ten years of age I was as familiarly acquainted with [Shakespeare's] lovers and his clowns, as with Robinson Crusoe, the Pilgrim's Progress, and the Bible. In later years I have left Robinson and the Pilgrim to the perusal of the children; but have continued to read the Bible and Shakespeare.

John Quincy Adams

The French military strategist Tranquier argues that propaganda control of mass media is essential in modern times. He was speaking of decolonization in Vietnam and Algeria but the same thesis applies to knowledge of events in Afghanistan, Iraq, Iran and beyond.

The worlds of the Bible, Shakespeare and Yogananda's teachings require effort to understand but are transforming, rather than simply entertaining in the manner of modern news sport-celebrity-movie programming. Along these lines, in present day Chile, a program is underway to send classics to the homes of even the most underprivileged child. Even in China, efforts are now underway to broaden the reading matter of school children.

Totalitarian regimes from Nazi Germany, to Soviet Russia, Socialist France and Communist North Korea always move first to control the school curriculum with little favor for books such as Hesse's "Siddhartha" or "Damian". A bright future, for them, involves party loyalty, working to pay taxes and despising anything beyond the barriers of official ideology.

Mass media forced reading into decline, yet the Internet is bringing back niche audiences for the specific and the profound. The research for this book benefited from the indexing abilities of Google yet is fundamentally based on the tens of works written by or derived from Yogananda and the Kriya Yoga Line of Gurus.

New Media for a New Age

Elinor Smith Sullivan, winner of the 1930 Best Woman Aviator of the Year Award, described the impact Lindbergh had on aviation with his transatlantic flight of 1927 (227 Dwapara)

"People seemed to think we [aviators] were from outer space or something. But after Charles Lindbergh's flight, we could do no wrong. It's hard to describe the impact Lindbergh had on people. Even the first walk on the moon doesn't come close. The twenties was such an innocent time, and people were still so religious - I think they felt like this man was sent by God to do this. And it changed aviation forever because all of a sudden the Wall Streeters were banging on doors looking for airplanes to invest in. We'd been standing on our heads trying to get them to notice us but after Lindbergh, suddenly everyone wanted to fly, and there weren't enough planes to carry them."

Lindbergh ushered in the age of aviation but was simultaneously the world's first superstar since the events coincided with a new optimism in America and a new power of media. It was into just this period that Yogananda stepped forth, forming his organization, SRF Inc., in the very home of the media industry in the Los Angeles of 1925.

Mount Washington, the site of his headquarters, had itself been a hotel, one of the main tourist attractions of the city, frequented by early movie stars such as Charlie Chaplin. Yogananda's main media technique for spreading the teachings was to replace the quiet, one-to-one approach of his guru and paramguru with modern publicity, public lectures, printed lessons with titles like "Super Advanced Course", a few magic tricks to engage audiences (stopping the pulse, having peoples hands stick to walls) and later an annual convention in Los Angeles' luxurious Biltmore Hotel. In his early years he had nearly gone broke following the traditional Indian methods, living meager meal to meager meal at a rented room in a Boston YMCA and reaching comparatively few people.

In that same innovative tradition Ananda (closely followed by Roy E. Davis) has the most creative use of new media, with inspirational online texts, articles, discourses, photos, music and even blogs, disseminating the teachings far beyond the reach of ordinary meetings, books or CDs.

It used to be that to learn a subject a mentor or personal tutor was required. To this day, this approach gives rise to genius in the world of classical music but if that were the only method, what would be left for the billions in full classrooms with ordinary teachers or those with neither classroom nor teacher?

Flying

After WWII, the limitations of the road, rail and river networks were already well known. The government in the US had grand plans to encourage all private individuals to fly. Planes such as the Ercoupe had their heyday.

Targeted at the non-professional pilot, the Ercoupe was also designed to be spin-proof with no

dangerous stall characteristics. Inexpensive to operate
and maintain, the Ercoupe was able to fly into and out
of small airfields, and its nose-wheel steering made
taxiing almost like driving an automobile. It was a
bold, Dwapara vision, building on Hoovers 1928 'Chicken
in every pot and a car in every garage' promise.

The vision lost more and more of its drive up
until today where the US government is contemplating
the same moves as Europe did decades ago: to keep the
skies for its richest sponsors: the industrial-military
complex with no place for the private individual.
Flight is a characteristic of the higher ages such as
Dwapara Yuga. Today, a solid second-hand airplane costs
less than a typical Sport Utility Vehicle, yet only 1/2
of one percent of Americans knows how to fly.

As early as 1900, based on his Dwapara Yuga
calculations, Swami Sri Yukteswar foresaw the
importance of flight to the New Age and predicted it
was to become an everyday occurrence per his biographer
Swami Satyananda. Churchward's 1931 "Children of Mu"
details his research on ancient aircraft:

"These are the most detailed accounts I have
found about the airships of the Hindus 15,000 to
20,000 years ago, except one which is a drawing
and instructions for the construction of the
airship and her machinery, power, engine, etc. The
power is taken from the atmosphere in a very
simple inexpensive manner. The engine is somewhat
like our present-day turbine in that it works from
one chamber into another until finally exhausted.
When the engine is once started it never stops
until turned off. It will continue on if allowed
to do so until the bearings are worn out. These
ships could keep circling around the earth without
ever once coming down until the machinery wore
out. The power is unlimited, or rather limited
only by what metals will stand.
I find various flights spoken of which
according to our maps would run from 1000 to 3000
miles. All records relating to these airships
distinctly state that they were self-moving, they
propelled themselves; in other words, they
generated their own power as they flew along. They
were independent of all fuel. It seems to me, in
the face of this, and with all our boasting, we
are about 15,000 to 20,000 years behind the times
. . . . There are many Chinese records of about the
same date regarding these ancient flying

machines." It is noteworthy that recent excavations in Crete have brought to light records which mention Cretan airplanes. "

As early as 1952, Wernher von Brown, the architect of Hitler's "V" weapons and America's successful missile and space exploration programs had proposed vehicles for a Mars Mission. This and many futuristic vehicles failed to take off, in part due to the success of the Moon Landings, the extreme cost and difficulty of succeeding them, the relative failure of the Shuttle and finally the loss of the Soviet Union as a funding impetus.

In parallel to the public "Space Race", the secret Corona Program of spy satellites gave America the confidence to have arms limitations talks with the Soviet Union (since facts on the ground were now verifiable) and ultimately lead to peace.

Intriguingly when we finally fully explore the planets of our Solar system we may find evidence of our having been there before since the cyclical nature of the Yugas implies that if we have the technology at a given point in time then we also had it in the past.

Space-conquering machines

Key turning points in the history of Dwapara Yuga have been associated with machinery that was characterized by a mastery of physical space. The German siege of Paris in 1870 (170 Dwapara) gave the world the word Communism ... and the people who lived it, rats to eat. One positive idea came from the events: effective travel and communication by air since the French creatively used balloons during the siege. American entered WWI, following a 'surprise' German submarine attack in 1915 on its ship RMS Lusitania.

Zeppelin, who had been present at the siege of Paris, was inspired to design his eponymous airships with a goal of linking distant peoples in a period before heavier-than-air flying machines. It was not to be, becoming instead a propaganda symbol of Nazi power. American had blockaded supplies of Helium, so instead they were filled with dangerous Hydrogen. In 1933, the Zeppelin Hindenberg exploded near New York City, a precursor of Germany's physical and technological defeat before America.

American entered WWII, following the 'surprise' attack on its naval base in Hawaii by Japanese planes from nearby aircraft carriers in 1941. WWIII was narrowly averted when Russia and America backed-down over missile deployments in Cuba and (less well known) Turkey in 1962.

The fictional scenario of the Terminator Series of movies (I to III) from 1984 (284 Dwapara) was computer-controlled weaponry engaging in what is euphemistically called 'friendly fire'. The scenario seems more and more likely to anyone familiar with today's computer-controlled battlefields and remotely guided, armed ground and aerial devices. As the action speeds up, more and more pressure is placed on commanders to remove human elements from the chain of command.

Yesterday's boy soldiers were trained in the Boy Scouts (which became the Hitler Youth in Germany and Austria with no change in program since the original aims were paramilitary). Today's soldiers are trained with war games on computers.

Science fiction tends to be little about science and more a commentary on present day social issues. Brave New World (1932) and 1984 (1948) certainly described scientific methods that came to be built - genetic manipulation and mass-surveillance - but their real commentary was on the totalitarian societies that used them to maintain their grip on power.

Future Technology

Dwapara is the age characterized by annihilation of space. We already have planes, trains, automobiles and ever-faster rockets and space ships and yet we are only at 307 Dwapara in an age that runs to 2400 Dwapara.

Logically a complete mastery would imply instant matter transport - teleportation. After all many of the other advances of Dwapara Yuga such as telescope, telegraph, radio and television exploiting sight and sound at a distance would have seemed miraculous in the Middle Ages. We have yet to fully understand touch, taste and smell at a distance. This will likely come as we explore the finer and finer positive, neutral and negative aspects of electricity, as the ancients described them.

The next age, Treta, beginning at 2400 Dwapara is characterized by mastery of time, so perhaps will give us time-travel. If Kali Yuga was symbolized by iron for swords and simple tools and Dwapara for Bronze, principally copper, for electricity, what will silver signify in Treta Yuga and gold in the still higher Satya Yuga?

The ancient Sanskrit writings of India describe amazing devices, used then, as presumably for the future, in both war and peace. The scientists of the Manhattan Atomic Bomb project described their invention in terms of the Vedas back in 245 Dwapara (1945). Today's scientists are beginning to look to these same ancient Indian Sanskrit documents for inspiration in the same way that the Renaissance scientists looked to their Greek counterparts, mirrored in time on either side of the 500 AD pit of Kali Yuga.

More and more archeological evidence is being uncovered of ancient planes, for example, plane-motif jewelry in South America and also fused buildings and radioactive skeletons at Mohenjo Daro in India, presumably from past nuclear war. As an obscure remnant of higher ages, today's black magic and its emphasis on spells recalls the (much more devastating) mantra or thought bombs used in the past higher ages. Yogananda described all of the above in his predictions.

In the same way that WWI and WWII cleared the old mentalities after the dawning of 0 Dwapara in 1900, for the atomic generations of 1946, 1966, 1986 and so on, so too will future wars clear the 'dead wood' for future ages and revelations.

New Barriers

The first police state was defined by Richelieu in France several centuries ago, characterized by networks of local informants and extensive documentation, a system still in place in modern France with a designated informant for each apartment building. The same ideas were seized by National and Communist Socialists from the 1930s and extensively refined by the French Army for its 50s colonial wars in Indo China and Algeria, then exported to the US-Vietnam conflict in the 60s and 70s and Latin American Dictatorships in the 70s and 80s.

Each of these led to horrible abuses and war crimes. High technology simply allows evil to happen faster, beginning with IBM Germany (officially taken over by Nazi regime) automating the Final Solution. One of the most chilling exhibits in Dachau Concentration Camp is the many bids and tenders from companies competing to improve (in full knowledge) the processes of evil. Krupps, Porsche and Hugo Boss have shed their Nazi past in modern-America, although one-time makers of gas ovens, tanks and SS uniforms.

The fall of the Soviet Union Provided a brief respite, with the excuse of the Cold War gone. Since 9/11, with newer electronic versions, the police states are back with a vengeance, this time with bloated budgets and little accountability for the 'War on Terror'. The UK has never relaxed its censorship of media, in the form of the D or now DA notice.

Movements there are followed by cellphone signal, images on CCTV, auto tags by 'traffic' cameras, DNA is vacuumed up and every trip, purchase, email and phone call analyzed by machine. The latest development is stealth drones indiscriminately surveying even concertgoers. The missile-enabled versions fly in Iraq and Afghanistan.

Dwapara is the breaking down of barriers, the above are a technically advanced form of Kali Yuga control - mass spying, justified by an unproven ability to catch terrorists whose very nature means they operate outside of normal society.

As Yogananda emphasized, the means color the ends, mass spying is not a way to catch terrorists. Instead good police work and human intel is the way to go, targeting would-be terrorists and not blanketing whole populations and over relying on technical gizmos that oppress the innocent rather than capturing the guilty.

> "Any society that would give up a little liberty to gain a little security will deserve neither and lose both."
> Benjamin Franklin

It is a rather ironic error that governments in wishing to "protect us" from whatever budget-filling, popularity enhancing "boogieman" they define or (in an historical sense) create, they instead become him. Aren't all-powerful, all-surveying, torturing states with little rule of law what we are seeking to avoid becoming?

Space Weather

With the dawning of Dwapara Yuga, the quantity and speed of delivery of information have both increased dramatically. It used to be print media transported by horseback, or truck (think of the inordinate importance given to newspapers in the "Superman" or "Spiderman" films), then radio ("Fireside chats") and then finally television broadcasts ("News-Entertainment-Sports"). CNN ushered in the satellite television a generation ago.

Today we have laptops and devices such as Smart Phones that instantly share global news and allow us to communicate with anyone anywhere. Adverse weather such as hurricanes, snowstorms and the like used to impede the physical transmission of newspapers, or drop television or radio networks.

Today, the vulnerability to the flow of information is space weather - solar wind. It periodically disables commercial satellites, overloads power grids and cuts wireless communications, including television, radio, GPS and cellphones not only for private citizens but emergency services and military communities.

Space weather forecasters predict increased activity thru to 2012, which is going to mean more interruptions. Ben Franklin is considered the father of modern weather forecasting. In World War II, weather forecasting was hugely important, for example fixing the date of the 1944 D-Day landings. In the failed attempt to liberate the Iranian hostages in 1979, weather proved the US's undoing (sand storms). In Dwapara, with satellites and communications blinded temporarily, solar weather may again prove decisive.

Subtle Energies

NRG Energy will shortly (2007) request permission to build two new nuclear reactors. It's the first request to build a new nuclear power plant in the U.S. in three decades. The Nuclear Regulatory Commission has geared up for a flood of applications. Decades of propaganda, lobbying and funding from Russia and the Middle East along with the well known accidents of Windscale (multiple) in the UK, Three Mile Island in the US and Chernobyl in the Ukraine made Europe and North America heavily dependent on oil.

Nuclear Energy can make a country self-sufficient, with France perhaps best exemplifying that. The world's advanced navies use nuclear engines for the same reasons, improbably championed by Jimmy Carter prior to becoming president.

Dwapara is all about discovering finer energies. The downside of nuclear fission, on which commercial plants are based, is the waste materials. Environmentalists are right to be concerned about these. The way forward is nuclear fusion, which generates energy but not the harmful wastes. Unfortunately such a technology upsets many powerful lobby groups, much as solar, wind and other energies and research has somewhat stalled.

Finding finer energies requires international cooperation. Recently the US canceled its Superconducting Super Collider in Northern Texas, after having spent over $2 billion on it. It seems the main reason was an unwillingness to share with foreign partners, who in turn were unwilling to share money. As in all alternate energies, Machiavellian political dimensions give an appearance of cooperation, money is disbursed but results are not obtained.

A similar facility, CERN, in Switzerland and France (located symbolically across the border region) has not only increased our knowledge of finer energies but spun off the World-wide-web as a by-product. In all things nuclear France is exemplar, the idea of big science fitting well with past Communist Socialist big plan thinking -- even a broken clock is right twice per day.

One hundred years ago, London, England (as opposed to Canada!) had the world's largest fleet of electric buses. It was commonly thought that they were a technological failure, beaten out by the petrol engine. In fact, they were far superior, so much so that they attracted fraud and the profits were stolen. That unfortunate incident tainted the progress for a hundred years.

Much as in the early work of Tesla and wireless electricity a 100 years ago, or the 150 years of knowledge of solar panels, it takes time for the popular consciousness to catch up with the minds of a few geniuses. At MIT, as of 2007, the Witricity team predicts another 3 to 5 years before wireless electricity is commercially available, although related "power pads" are just now beginning to reach the early adopter market.

The challenge of solar and wind energy today is the difficulty of marketing such new concepts to the general public beyond the environmentalist and hitech folk, who are already convinced and have such systems. The larger public wants simple, affordable systems that will be maintenance free and add to the values of their homes and lifestyles, rather than the current 'expensive science project' state of affairs with every install supposedly a heavily customized, one-off affair.

International, co-operative endeavors into finding finer energies are destined to succeed since they ride the wave of Dwapara Yuga. Its exemplar, Ben Franklin, gave away the patent of the Franklin stove, so that all America might be heated. Now is the time to be able light and heat the whole world, stripping away the greed of certain lobbies tied into Kali Yuga ways of extracting huge profits and thoughtlessly contaminating the environment. It was once 'a car in every garage and a chicken in every pot' that might become 'fly from every garage, power from water (fusion) and organic fruits and vegetables in every plot.'

Diet

A surprising number of the people featured in the timeline are vegetarians, the dietary restrictions helping them to tune into the ideas of the age. Yogananda explains, "Thoughts are universally and not individually rooted."

- Writers: Tolstoy and Thoreau
- Scientists: Da Vinci, Ben Franklin, Edison, Einstein and Tesla
- Politicians: Ben Franklin, Gandhi and Hitler

Many more add fish, for example Steve Jobs of Apple, or poultry, essentially avoiding the most damaging red meat. Yogananda ascribed the sweet taste of pork to the amount of puss it contains. Yogananda quotes Sri Yukteswar in the "Autobiography of a Yogi":

"My guru was a vegetarian. Before embracing monkhood, however, he had eaten eggs and fish. His advice to students was to follow any simple diet which proved suited to one's constitution."

The healthiest groups in the US are Adventists and LDS (Mormon), with the latter less so given their diets, which more closely mirror (unhealthy) US norms. Adventists advocate vegetarianism and discourage members from the use of alcohol, tobacco or illegal drugs. In addition, some Adventists avoid coffee and other beverages containing caffeine. LDS (Mormon)'s "Word of Wisdom" suggests avoiding alcohol, drugs, tea and coffee but also meat, although many (so-called "Jack") members ignore this advice.

Yogananda was one of several Indians who wrote articles for Benedict Lust's "Nature's Path" in the 1920's, gaining wide exposure to a large American audience. Lust was harassed by authorities and medical associations for promoting natural methods of healing, massage and nude sun bathing at his health resorts. In terms of diet, Yogananda was one of the first to warn against the dangers of cigarettes, alcohol and red meat. He also warned against fanaticism in diet since many of the SRF Inc. nuns and monks were needlessly strict on diet to the detriment of their health. This was said to be a factor in Saint Lynn's early death.

Music

Everything is vibration, Aum, or the word of God. Perhaps more so than any other medium, music captures something of what is behind our material world. In traditional Indian music, the phenomenon is so well captured that a night raga played in the day by a true adept can make the sky become dark. Something of this can be heard in the raga-influenced music of Led Zeppelin.

In the twentieth century music has defined each age. Even a snippet of music makes even the most hardened heart think back to a first love, dear friend or relative, capable of raising emotions from anger to spiritual ardor. Movies and books somehow lose their power with age yet music retains its vital spark and mystique.

There appears to be a subtle link to reincarnation with musical ability even in the most humble child and poorest circumstances leading to worldwide fame and reward, from Elvis to Ozzy Osborne. In the negative onslaught that was the French Revolution, the revolutionaries moved quickly to seize the land and monies of the church and aristocracy before setting themselves in their place (with appropriate new vocabularies of citizen and the like). A particular target was church bells, not for their worth but to suppress the tuned effect of them had on the populace. Bells are one of the least studied and yet most widely heard of all instruments.

In modern France, there is a greater familiarity with the Tibetan music that mimics the sound of the body than what once was the original sound of the cathedrals. Yogananda's music and the vibration it carries survives the many edits of his pictures and written works that the Mata Regime made. In his original preface to the book "Cosmic Chants", Yogananda wrote:

"Each of these Cosmic Chants has been composed to satisfy a special need of mind or life. The devotee's various moods and inner desires can be strengthened or changed by the repetition of one particular chant suitable for that purpose. "

In Dwapara Yuga, the most advanced technologies are lasers and sonic drills, phenomena of vibration. As older monuments are being analyzed it is being discovered that their amazingly precise dimensions were achieved this way, typically to reflect some astronomical verity such as the progress of the Yugas.

The Network

Al Queda means "The Network". Its goals are to build a large Muslem state, ruled on the lines of middle ages Califs - literally to roll back time one thousand years. For our post 9/11 era, it is the latest manifestation of retrogressive Kali Yuga influence, after the National and Communist Socialism movements that starved, murdered and mentally enslaved millions last century.

The differences are many, "The Network" is not a country, book, or even large number of people rather a brand and vague idea that unites, in terminology at least, disgruntled elements, not in its vision for the future but violence and murder.

Most revolutions topple one regime for a similar regime with a new vocabulary, e.g. Imperial Czars became Communist Dictators became Capitalist Dictators in the case of Russia. That would seem to be the real goal of "the Network" to seize power in the Middle East, changing names but carrying on just the same and pocketing the oil dollars themselves.

Fidel Castro in Cuba seized power and wanted to clamp down on the prostitution and bars that had come to define the island, almost immediately he had to back down and continue as before, an iron hand over a sad tourist economy. He and his brother kept the money. From the opposite side of the spectrum, General Pinochet in Chile seized power to save the country from Communist Dictatorship, continued much as before and, of course, kept the money in Swiss accounts.

The US Revolution is one of the rarest, removing the old problems and founding a better society, although it too has a tendency to replicate the old British system of hereditary kingship and rule by wealthy elite. The US is fighting an old-style war in Iraq, as has been noted from the 50's onwards, the real battle is one of hearts and minds out on the Internet.

Yogananda pointed out that the means influence the ends. Violent means lead to violent ends. Democracy at gunpoint is a self-defeating school of thought. Real change is in a societal sense can be reached constructively with schools, hospitals, jobs and prosperity. That does not mean that self-defensive wars, or those limiting the aggression of rogue states are wrong per se. The greatest reform is not of others but of oneself.

Soft Power

France has had its Alliance Francaise since 1883 pushing French ideas and culture around the world. (Remember Sri Yukteswar initially wrote the Holy Science in French). Britain has had its British Council since 1934, with similar British aims. Other similar institutions are Società "Dante Alighieri" (Italy), Goethe Institut (Germany), Instituto Cervantes (Spain) and Instituto Camões (Portugal).

America never really needed these in the sense that movies, radio, television and novels provided that for free. Up until the Iraq occupation, America was widely admired. What it is discovering is that in Dwapara Yuga, positive messages are much more effective and less expensive than bullets and bombs.

Russia has learned that lesson too and has begun its own program of Russian culture, reaching out to the ex Warsaw Pact states. The hippies had something after all, putting flowers in guns in the Summer of Love.

Russia and the US are discovering that a Dwapara Yuga way forward is Tennessee Williams and Dostoevsky rather than M16s and AK47s. Ideas are powerful things, much more powerful than any weapons platform or goose-stepping surveillance operatives.

Empowering individuals

According to the original "stone soup" story, some travelers come to a village, carrying nothing more than an empty pot. Upon their arrival, the villagers are unwilling to share any of their food stores with the hungry travelers. The travelers fill the pot with water, drop a large stone in it, and place it over a fire in the village square. One of the villagers becomes curious and asks what they are doing. The travelers answer that they are making "stone soup", which tastes wonderful, although it still needs a little bit of garnish to improve the flavor, which they are missing.

The villager doesn't mind parting with just a little bit to help them out, so it gets added to the soup. Another villager walks by, inquiring about the pot, and the travelers again mention their stone soup, which hasn't reached its full potential yet. The villager hands them a little bit of seasoning to help them out. More and more villagers walk by, each adding another ingredient. Finally, a delicious and nourishing pot of soup is enjoyed by all. The stone may or may not be reused in the next soup, and fortunately is not eaten.

In Kali Yuga, the sponsorship of powerful elites - kings, nobles, rich merchants, trade unionists or party officials was required for everything. Today, with technology and a prevailing wind of expansive Dwapara Yuga, individuals and groups all possess a magic stone to make any project a reality.

Empowered Minorities

A native of Mumbai, Azim Premji has tapped India's abundant engineering talent to transform a family vegetable-oil firm, Wipro Ltd., into a technology and outsourcing giant. By serving Western manufacturers, airlines and utilities, the company has brought Mr. Premji a fortune of some $17 billion -- believed to be greater than that of any other Muslim outside of Persian Gulf royalty. Three events played into this:

- 1947 Partition - Mr. Premji's family did not define themselves along religious lines and leave for Pakistan

- 1977 Communist Socialists clamped down on multinationals, prompting the exodus of corporate giants like International Business Machines Corp. and Coca-Cola Co. Mr. Premji and others stepped in, beginning to manufacture computers and other electronics.

- 2000 Year 2000 myth drove huge business for Wipro, Tata and Infosys from the USA and Europe

India has the largest Muslim population in the world, after Pakistan and Indonesia. Interestingly, the Tata industrialist family, are Parsi, followers of the Zoroastrian Iranian faith. Freddie Mercury of the group Queen (Farrokh Bulsara) was probably the most famous Parsi in the West. The success of minorities in India has a number of parallels with the success of Jewish people in America.

Bill Gates (Microsoft), Larry Ellison (Oracle) and Steve Jobs (Apple, Pixar, Disney) in the US have been mentioned often in this book. Both Jobs and Ellison were adopted. The LDS (Mormon) Church, which began with its leader being murdered by a mob and whose home state, Utah, only joined the United States under threat of war, is now the richest religion in the US per capita, with a credible shot at taking the presidency of the United States with Mitt Romney. SRF Inc., which at one stage was so poor that members survived on eating home grown tomatoes, is now one of the wealthiest institutions in the US. Dwapara Yuga is characterized by the breaking down of barriers.

Three rings - family, work and community

An individual participates in family groups, at work (whether in fields, factories or now the new factories of professions) and in the community (organized religion, schools, colleges, nations, races etc.). Throughout ascending Dwapara Yuga, we can see individuals throwing off the shackles of group thought (and karma) in community, in work and finally the family group to become themselves not in outward identification but inward reflection.

> "I tell you the truth," Jesus replied, "no one who has left home or brothers or sisters or mother or father or children or fields for me and the gospel will fail to receive a hundred times as much in this present age (homes, brothers, sisters, mothers, children and fields—and with them, persecutions) and in the age to come, eternal life. But many who are first will be last, and the last first."
> Mark 29

> "Mind, nor intellect, nor ego, feeling;
> Sky nor earth nor metals am I.
> I am He, I am He, Blessed Spirit, I am He!
> No birth, no death, no caste have I;
> Father, mother, have I none.
> I am He, I am He, Blessed Spirit, I am He!
> Beyond the flights of fancy, formless am I,
> Permeating the limbs of all life;
> Bondage I do not fear; I am free, ever free,
> I am He, I am He, Blessed Spirit, I am He!"
> Sanskrit chant of Lord Shankara

One of the most powerful techniques of corporate, religious and political cults is combining the three rings of family, work and community to bind individuals more powerfully to the 'beloved leaders', rather than letting the rings drop naturally of themselves.

> "One Ring to rule them all, One Ring to find them, One Ring to bring them all and in the darkness bind them"
> Lord of the rings, Tolkien

Karma and transgenerational therapy

Jaime Delgadillo Miranda writes:

> "Transgenerational phenomena concern the transmission and exchange of cultural affaires, wherein the individual psychological experience is intimately related to and influenced by the complex web of relationships within the family/social structure. This cultural inheritance, which comprises the mobility of values, ideals, interdictions, mandates, and such aspects from previous generations to the latter, immerses the human - biological - subject within an orderly dimension of exchanges and relation."

This new discipline is primarily known and written about outside of the English Language, with strong poles in Latin America and Europe. Anne Utzenberger, in one of the few English language titles, "Ancestor Syndrome: Transgenerational Psychotherapy and the Hidden Links in the Family Tree", shows:

> "As mere links in a chain of generations, we may have no choice in having the events and traumas experienced by our ancestors visited upon us in our own lifetime. The book includes fascinating case studies to illustrate how her clients have conquered seemingly irrational fears, psychological and even physical difficulties by discovering and understanding the parallels between their own life and the lives of their forebears. The theory of "invisible loyalty" owed to previous generations, which may make us unwittingly re-enact their life events, is discussed in the light of ongoing research into transgenerational therapy."

The above authors are continuing a tradition from Freud and Jung of exploring the inner self, a science that was perfected by the ancient Yogis and passed down to us by, amongst others, the Kriya Yoga Line of Gurus. A more Yogic explanation of the transgenerational phenomena is that our individual karma attracts us to be born in families, groups, races and societies in tune with our natures.

Our documented past can be relatively easily be found through conventional geneology. However, that does not capture past family traumas, or even past family scandal, still less our own past lives. Modern

DNA techniques can establish blood-lineages and even to which groups we are historically related. Many individuals, particularly if they have spiritual tendencies, might also find their lives recorded in the "Book of Brighu."

Much as the position of the stars at the first breath (astrology), the constellation of family and societal contacts suggest the path an individual will take if no spiritual effort is made. Precious metals and stones worn next to the skin, knowledge coming down to us (much as the Book of Brighu) from higher ages, can to an extent outwit the stars (or family constellation). The more sure method is Kriya Yoga, burning the karmic seed tendencies of this and previous lives.

Much as organizational leaders are not like the office workers, civil servants or soldiers they command, the great good and bad leaders resemble each other in their (public) certainty of vision and capacity to inspire mass followings. The more successful a person is politically, financially and socially, the greater their capacity for the general good and self-improvement, or evil, in misusing that power, capable of being either a Gandhi or a Hitler.

The Internet

The Internet is a manifestation of Dwapara Yuga, breaking time and space to give instant access to knowledge and near instant access to products and services around the globe. It can drive good; for example, help groups around rare diseases, or evil in connecting terrorists. It can connect one to the most beautiful thoughts or vilest portrayal of torture. To paraphrase Yogananda, better to concentrate on the flowers in a beautiful garden than search the gutters for dirt. Kriyananda wrote:

> "Every thought form has its own magnetism. The more we invest a thought with energy, the greater its magnetic hold on us. One can be drawn into any delusion by simply concentrating on it, and investing it with energy. The satanic force is not some sly, shifty-eyed imp with horns, hooves, and a long tail.
>
> Satan, Yogananda explained, is an aspect of infinite consciousness itself. God, in creating the universe, manifested an infinite number of thought forms, each of them a vortex, itself, of consciousness and energy. Thus, each thought form

generates its own magnetism. "Satan" is that force which consciously draws one into the ideational vortex of one's choice, and prevents him from releasing his awareness and letting it expand toward infinity. "

Many people have remarked in college and in society in general that those who become overly enamored of computers and the Internet become slaves to them, becoming diminished socially, mentally and physically while imagining the opposite to be the case.

In most tech companies, the executives are aware of the potential of technology but are not owned by it. Those who are consumed form the lowest ranks: they are not made victims, they make themselves victims. The Internet is not Satanic or Mayic per se, rather it is an amplifier, it can take the smallest weakness and make it huge, conversely it can take the smallest glimmer of talent or positive direction and make it a life's work. It is all a question of which vrittis in the spine are activated.

Digital Freedom

One of the most evident signs of Dwapara Yuga is the Internet - breaking down barriers, sharing knowledge and connecting people. Its foundations were international standards and open-source software, i.e. that permits users to use, change, improve and to redistribute it in modified or unmodified form. Open source is often developed in a public, typically international and collaborative manner, much akin to user-generated content such as wikipedia. It can also be commercial as well, for example, in products such as Alfresco or MySQL with revenues coming from subscriptions for support rather than so-called licenses and maintenance. Its ideas are in tune with the New Age. It is typically known and used by highly educated young people.

The flip side of the coin is hugely capitalized companies such as Microsoft, Oracle and SAP that although beginning as innovators with huge value, grew so massive that they now simply seek to corner their markets, raise prices and slow innovation becoming the monopolistic equivalents of the old AT&T or Standard Oil that stifled competition and overcharged customers last century (and this in the case of AT&T and its "Baby Bells").

Their business interests are to slow progress and have every inching step forward paid for to them (license upgrades), a very Kali Yuga exploitative model, much admired by politicians bought with lobby dollars or well-catered-to journalists with an eye to advertising dollars.

The poster child of innovation in the face of monopolists is Firefox, whose free open source browser runs on Windows, Macs and Linux and has no hidden agenda of locking-users in, as does Microsoft's "Internet Explorer". Lock-in is in the nature of proprietary software, it may begin free but once it reaches dominance the feature means there is no possibility of competition or simple change. Historically IBM invented the strategy, which is now aped by Microsoft (which collaborated on operating systems and then betrayed IBM), Oracle (which stole IBM's ideas and after seven versions made its database product work) and SAP (which simply evolved from IBM in Germany). In India, Wipro, Infosys and Tata grew in IT by filling the void left by IBM when the Communist government forced the American giant out of the country.

One solution has been the European approach where very slowly Microsoft's anti competitive nature is being exposed. However, that great wealth buys great lawyers and publicity so the approach is both slow and competitors such as Netscape have long been run out of business. In the meantime, the public continues to be overcharged.

Another solution, typified by Firefox, is not by fighting monopolies with their own weapons - propaganda and expensive legal teams - but rather fighting them where they would prefer least to be fought, in terms of innovation, imagination and great quality - open source projects. A small international team of bright individuals, given an even playing field, can beat an army of corporate workers with their emphasis on formal qualifications and numbing conformity -- don't be fooled earrings, crocs and tattoos are just as much a uniform as suits were a generation ago -- freedom is in the mind not just clothing.

In terms of content, Wikipedia is both free and better than Microsoft's proprietary Encarta Encyclopedia and the venerable Encyclopedia Britannica. For commercial reasons, every country version of Encarta is different, telling each country what it wants to hear rather than what is actually true. Similarly, Microsoft, Yahoo and Google have collaborated with Chinese authorities to either limit content or in the case of Yahoo to reveal identities of dissidents.

Even Apple, which continues to innovate (since outside of iPods it is far from a monopoly), sells iTunes videos in the US which are not available/will not play in Europe thanks to excessively strict digital rights management (DRM). This is being challenged in the French Courts. This is the newest version of DVD regions that made people around the world wait for the out of date movie studios in Hollywood to move from Zone 1 to 2 etc in international distribution, artificially slowing progress.

DVD regions are ignored in open-source players and rigidly enforced in machines such as Apple computers, with their heavy partnership with Pixar/Disney. Open source collaborations are free and lively yet they have a little known Achilles heal - where to keep the collaboration in the real world before the companies have reached a mass market. In fact it happens in a little known University in Oregon on a charity rackathon basis. This makes sense when we examine that the great growth of knowledge since Dwapara has come from free sharing of scientific knowledge in universities.

The menace to that is patents and proprietary software not as a protection for inventors but for monopolies to maintain their markets and stifle both progress and the public, ideally locking people in to buying and re-buying the same old stuff in the way that the public was conned into buying the same songs on vinyl, then cassette, then 8-track, then CD and now DVD and iTunes.

In the 60s protesters were in the streets, today in line with New Age consciousness, its on the 'net. All the US Presidential candidates are playing this angle, fully informed of the psycho-demographics of Generation Y, as opposed to the Baby Boomers who are now retirees and defenders of out-of-date status quos, with pamphlets and badges of yesterday's organizations.

Enlightened countries such as India and Brazil are fully leveraging the open source movement so as not to continue as dollar-slaves to foreign masters. Dwapara's rising consciousness will eventually win out, that does not mean the battle will not be hard fought with many reverses.

Conclusion

Yogananda's teachings unify the best of the East and the West. The spiritual, family and business success of householder saints such as Lahiri Mahasaya, Swami Sri Yukteswar, Yogananda's father, Dr. Lewis, Saint Lynn and Yogacharya Oliver Black testify to the effectiveness of the teachings. As Jesus said, by the fruit we know the tree. The teachings are a culmination of the ideas of many great men and women in the East and West, living on in their original form, as well as a myriad of offshoots. In this fertile soil, Dwapara Yuga will continue to flower.

Yogananda and Sri Yukteswar practiced meditation, vigorous sports and martial arts, careful not to follow the examples of "bloodless pedants", with mere book learning. Sri Yukteswar emphasized that an individual must manifest all of the virtues of a priest, a warrior, a merchant and a servant to others[30] to be considered a success. The author leaves the last words to Yogananda and his vision of a United States of the World from the "Autobiography of a Yogi":

> "'World' is a large term, but man must enlarge his allegiance, considering himself in the light of a world citizen. A person who truly feels: 'The world is my homeland; it is my America, my India, my Philippines, my England, my Africa,' will never lack scope for a useful and happy life. His natural local pride will know limitless expansion; he will be in touch with creative universal currents."

---

[30] These are the categories of Manu's system of human characteristics that became ossified into the caste system in India.

Kriya Yoga Line of Gurus

It was said that Yogananda cast a wide net, using modern marketing and publicity to attract as many people as possible. He is certainly the most well known of all the teachers in the Kriya Yoga Line of Gurus. The lists below show the relationships from Lahiri to Sri Yukteswar to Yogananda to those direct disciples still living such as Swami Kriyananda and Roy E. Davis.

Essentially only one long branch and a few leaves are shown from a mighty trunk with many branches. The author does not intend to promote one branch or leaf over any other, merely showing the relationships to each other. The apt researcher will find much discussion between the branches over the merits of American style marketing and publicity and the simplifications of the practices and techniques for a broad audience. Fame and renown have certain monetary benefits and there is a certain amount of jostling for being the "most authentic". Discrimination is left to the reader.

What seems clear to the author is that each guru showed the divine light according to the lens of his nature, for example, in devotion with Yogananda and Satyananda and in a dryer, more scientific manner for Sri Yukteswar and Dhirananda.

Mahavatar Babaji guru of:
• Swami Lahiri Mahasaya

Swami Lahiri Mahasaya guru of:
• Panchanan Bhattacharya (founded Aryya Mission Institution)
• Swami Mahabir
• Swami Kebalananda
• Swami Pranabananda
• Brahmachari Kesavananda
• Tinkori Lahiri
• Dukori Lahiri
• Swami Sri Yukteswar (founded Sadhu Sabha and Satsanga Sabha)
• Brajalal Adhikari
• Prasad Das Goswami
• Kali Kumar Banerjee
• Kesav Chandra Banerjee
• Ram Dayal Mazumder

- Hari Narayan Palodhi
- Bhupendranath Sanyal
- Brajalal Adhikari
- Joyram Bhattacharya
- Ramarupa Bhattacharya
- Kailash Chandra Benerjee
- Kanti Acharya

Swami Sri Yukteswar guru of:
- Motilal Mukherjee
- Swami Satyananda (initiated by Kebalananda, faithful to the end)
- Swami (later) Paramhansa Yogananda
- (founded YSS Inc., Ranchi School and SRF Inc.)
- Swami Bhabananda Giri
- Swami Paramananda
- Swami Narayana
- Amulya Charan Santra
- Bijoy Kumar Chatterjee
- Bipin Chandra Bhumia
- Swami Dhirananda (initiated by Kebalananda, left SRF Inc.)
- Sri Sailendra Bejoy Das Gupta
- Golakananda Giri
- Dasarathi Chatterjee

Paramhansa Yogananda guru of:
- Swami Atmananda
- Swami Sevananda
- Swami Sadananda
- Swami Binayananda
- Swami Bidyananda
- Swami Satchidananda
- Swami Premananda
  (left SRF Inc., founded Self-Revelation Church)
- Swami Kriyananda (left SRF Inc., founded Ananda)
- Swami Hariharananda (founded Kriya Yoga Institute)

Yogananda explicitly said there would be no gurus in the SRF Inc./YSS Inc. line and that the writings would be the guru, when he was gone. SRF Inc. and YSS Inc. provide heavily censored versions of his books.

Original works can be found from Ananda[31] and lessons from the Dallas Amrita Foundation[32]. Further material can be found via Yoga Niketan[33].

Some notable Yogananda disciples and their dates of first meeting him are:

- 1920 Boston, Dr. Lewis - First US Devotee
- 1924 San Francisco, Tara Mata – Yogananda's editor
- 1930 Detroit, Yogacharya Oliver Black (left SRF Inc., founded Song of the morning) - Second most advanced male devotee
- 1931 Salt Lake City, Daya Mata, her sister, Ananda Mata, mother and brother, Richard Wright – have controlled SRF Inc. since 1955
- 1932 Kansas, Rajarsi Janakananda - Most advanced male devotee, President after Yogananda's death, until his own in 1955
- 1947 Los Angeles, Norman Paulsen
  (left SRF Inc., founded Sunburst)
- 1948 Los Angeles, Swami Kriyananda
  (left SRF Inc., founded Ananda)
- 1949 Los Angeles, Roy Davis
  (left SRF Inc., founded Center for Spiritual Awareness)

A complete list would be huge; the diaspora of SRF Inc. ex Nuns and ex Monks has grown by over fifty in just the last ten years. Many of the ex Monastics in turn form organizations and so on. One of the earliest spin offs was by Hamid Bey. Either directly, through his books, or through followers, Yogananda (and his gurus)'s influence on the West has been huge.

Even such seemingly mainstream authors as JD Salinger were influenced by the teachings. The reader is cautioned against assuming that an organizational role or (more commonly in the US) ex-organizational role is a guarantee of enlightenment.

---

[31] Ananda.org
[32] amrita.com
[33] yoganiketan.net

Major Kriya Yoga Organizations in the United States

Ananda	ananda.org
Center for Spiritual Awareness	csa-davis.org
Kriya Yoga Institute	kriya.org
Self-Revelation church	self-revelationchurch.org
Song of the Morning	goldenlotus.org
SRF Inc.	srf-yogananda.org
Sunburst	sunburstonline.org

Bibliography

1894 The Holy Science by Swami Sri Yukteswar
1933 Astrological World Cycles by Tara Mata
1936 A Search in Secret India by Paul Brunton
1946 Autobiography of a Yogi by Paramhansa Yogananda
1947 Complete Works of Swami Vivekananda
1953 The worldly philosophers by Robert Heilbroner
1956 Books that changed the world by Robert Downs
1964 Modern Warfare by Roger Trinquier
1969 Priceless Precepts by Kamala Silva
1973 The Road Ahead by Swami Kriyananda
1980 Christ Consciousness by Norman Paulsen
1985 The Gospel of Sri Ramakrishna by Swami Nikhilananda "M"
1990 Liar's Poker: Rising Through the Wreckage on Wall Street by Michael Lewis
1991 Treasures Against Time by Brenda Lewis
1992 The Spiritual Seekers Guide by Steven S. Sadleir
1993 Trilogy of Divine Love by Durga Mata
1995 Secret of the Veda by Sri Aurobindo
1996 Divine Romance by Yogananda
1997 Remote Viewers: The Secret History of America's Psychic Spies by Jim Schnabel
2000 Journey to self-realization by Yogananda
2001 Autobiography of a spiritually incorrect mystic by Osho
2001 When Genius Failed: The Rise and Fall of Long-Term Capital Management by Roger Lowenstein
2002 Out of the Labyrinth by Swami Kriyananda
2002 The Tipping Point by Malcolm Gladwell
2004 The Palgrave companion to North American Utopias
2004 Way of the warrior by Reid and Croucher
2006 The Essence of the Bhagavad Gita by Swami Kriyananda
2006 The World Is Flat by Thomas Friedman
2006 Paramhansa Yogananda Life Portrait and Reminiscences by Sri Sailendra Bejoy Dasgupta
2006 A Collection of Biographies of four Kriya Yoga Gurus by Swami Satyananda
2007 Revelations of Christ by Swami Kriyananda

About the author

Friends from around the World:

The author is a student of the Yugas, met with many direct disciples of Paramhansa Yogananda, followers of Swami Sri Yukteswar and Swami Kebalananda in Europe, the US and India. Trained in physics, meeting Stephen Hawking and Richard Dawkins, and business, meeting many dot com and Wall Street leaders. The views expressed herein are the personal and not-for-profit views of the author and are not intended to reflect the views of any other individual or organization. A debt of gratitude is owed to Swami Kriyananda for the exceptional clarity of his writings and to the Kriya Yoga Line of Gurus who made this knowledge available in this New Age.

Poor Richard

Texas, USA
December, 307 Dwapara

Dwaparayuga.com

About this book

From the fall of Rome, around 500 AD, to the Renaissance, ten to twelve centuries later, almost nothing new was discovered. Man looked back to the great learning of classical civilization for inspiration: admiring their thinkers and architects but incapable of equaling them. In turn, those ancients looked back further, to a previous "Golden Age." Why did civilization fall and then rise again? In 1920, the Indian Yogi Paramhansa Yogananda, author of the spiritual classic "Autobiography of a Yogi", came to the United States with the answer.

Yogananda became the most popular speaker in the country, having the ear of leading figures such as the President, the Governor of California, Burbank, Ford and Edison. He brought an ancient message of simple living and high thinking to a new audience, emphasizing healthy diet, exercise and meditation at a time when these ideas were far from common.

Yogananda explained that we are entering a New Age called Dwapara Yuga characterized by a breakdown of the idea of a material world and a growing consciousness of the underlying unity of peoples, energy and nature. Like the days and years, the Yuga or Age is a natural, astronomical cycle in which civilization gradually rises for 12,000 years and then gradually falls for 12,000 years, as our Sun orbits its binary star. The ancient Indians called these ages Kali, Dwapara, Treta and Satya. The ancient Greeks called them Iron, Bronze, Silver and Gold.

In the period of 1600 to 1900 AD we transitioned from the constrictive, materialistic Kali Yuga or Iron Age to the expansive, energy-focused Dwapara Yuga or Bronze Age. This has lead to a continuing breakdown of barriers from oligarchy to democracy, serfdom and slavery to individual freedom and to inventions such as the telescope, television, atomic power, flight and the Internet. The subject of this short book is the unfolding Dwapara Yuga, Paramhansa Yogananda, his mission, those who inspired him and those who he inspired.